T0274846

# Arid Empire

# Arid Empire

## The Entangled Fates of
## Arizona and Arabia

Natalie Koch

VERSO

London • New York

*Dedicated to the Tohono O'odham,*
*whose lands gave me life*

—

First published by Verso 2022
© Natalie Koch 2022

1 3 5 7 9 10 8 6 4 2

**Verso**
UK: 6 Meard Street, London W1F 0EG
US: 388 Atlantic Avenue, Brooklyn, NY 11217
versobooks.com

Verso is the imprint of New Left Books

ISBN-13: 978-1-83976-369-4
ISBN-13: 978-1-83976-372-4 (US EBK)
ISBN-13: 978-1-83976-371-7 (UK EBK)

**British Library Cataloguing in Publication Data**
A catalogue record for this book is available from the British Library

**Library of Congress Cataloging-in-Publication Data**
A catalog record for this book is available from the Library of Congress

Typeset in Sabon by MJ & N Gavan, Truro, Cornwall
Printed by CPI Group (UK) Ltd, Croydon CR0 4YY

# Contents

# Acknowledgments

This book was made possible by many friends and colleagues in Arizona and the Arabian Peninsula whom I cannot name. I am grateful to them for opening their homes and their hearts to me and my idiosyncratic curiosity in the winding tales recounted here. I am also grateful to many others who patiently listened and read versions of this text and other writing from this project, including Todd Scheske, Andrew Curley, John Peterson, Victoria Hightower, Matt MacLean, Feras Klenk, Shaundel Sanchez, Francisco Robles, Meredith DeBoom, Neha Vora, Toby Jones, Chris Low, Gökçe Günel, Irina Kholkina, Barry Hashimoto, Georgi Derluguian, Steve Uyeda, JodyLee Duek, Jake Levine, Connie Greenberg, Chris Scott, Mike Pasqualetti, Beth Mitchneck, Annika Mattissek, and, as always, Ingrid Nelson. I had the pleasure of thinking through deserts with a group of students in my ARC/GEO 500 "Geopolitics of Deserts" seminar at Syracuse University, who helped me grasp the importance of finding an engaging approach to telling the story of arid empire. I also thank Joe Stoll in Syracuse Geography for creating the maps in this book. At Verso, I had the privilege of working with Jessie Kindig, whose perceptive and brilliant editing helped me to sharpen my arguments; her work was a tremendous contribution to making this book what it is.

Since I began this project in December 2018, I have had the chance to present some of my initial ideas and findings in many places. I am indebted to my many colleagues and friends who have given me feedback at these presentations, including Notre Dame's "Desert Futures: Sahara/Sonora" collective workshop; Yale University's Council on Middle East Studies; Syracuse University's Department of Geography and the Environment; Sierra Club Arizona; Arizona Hydrological Society; the Arizona Historical Society, the Leiden Institute for Area Studies' Workshop, "Circuits of Production, Crisis and Revolt: The Environment and Capital in the Middle East and North Africa"; University of North Carolina–Chapel Hill's Department of Geography; University of North Carolina–Greensboro's Department of Geography, Environment, and Sustainability; Duke University's Franklin Center for International and Global Studies; Sunnyside High School, Arizona State University's School of Geographical Sciences & Urban Planning; and the University of Arizona's Udall Center for Studies in Public Policy.

Select parts of this book have been published previously, and I am grateful to many colleagues for their feedback and contributions to honing my ideas in this earlier work. I developed parts of chapter 2 in "The Desert as Laboratory: Science, State-Making, and Empire in the Drylands, *Transactions of the Institute of British Geographers* 46, no. 2 (2021): 495–509; chapter 3 in "Desert Geopolitics: Arizona, Arabia, and an Arid-Lands Response to the Territorial Trap," *Comparative Studies of South Asia, Africa and the Middle East* 41, no. 1 (2021): 88–105; chapter 4 in "Agtech in Arabia: 'Spectacular Forgetting' and the Technopolitics of Greening the Desert," *Journal of Political Ecology* 26, no. 1 (2019): 666–86; and "The Political Lives of Deserts," *Annals of the American Association of Geographers* 111, no. 1 (2021): 87–104; chapter 5 in "Whose Apocalypse? Biosphere 2 and the Spectacle of Settler Science in the Desert," *Geoforum* 124 (2021): 36–45.

The research for this book was generously supported by the Fulbright Middle East and North Africa Regional Research Program; an Alexander von Humboldt Foundation Fellowship for Experienced Researchers; a CUSE Grant from the Syracuse University Office of Sponsored Programs; and a Social Sciences Research Council Transregional Research Junior Scholar Fellowship Consolidation Grant. Any opinions presented here are entirely my own, and do not reflect the views of any of these sponsors.

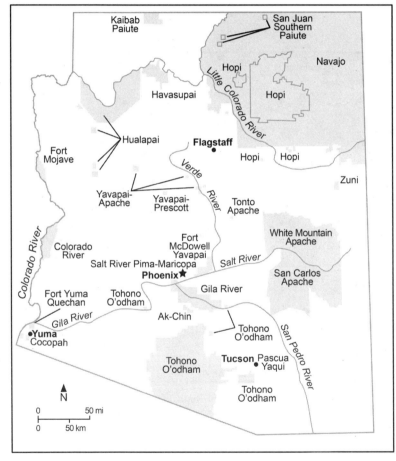

Kaibab
Paiute

San Juan
Southern
Paiute

Navajo

Little Colorado River

Hopi

Hopi

Havasupai

Fort
Mojave

Hualapai

**Flagstaff**

Hopi      Hopi

Zuni

Verde River

Yavapai-
Apache

Yavapai-
Prescott

Tonto
Apache

White Mountain
Apache

Colorado
River

Colorado River

Fort
McDowell
Yavapai

Salt River Pima-Maricopa

**Phoenix**★

Salt River

San Carlos
Apache

Fort Yuma
Quechan

Tohono
O'odham

Gila River

Gila River

Ak-Chin

Tohono
O'odham

San Pedro River

•**Yuma**
Cocopah

Tohono
O'odham

**Tucson** Pascua
• Yaqui

▲
N

Tohono
O'odham

0        50 mi

0        50 km

*Contemporary Arizona.*

*Source:* Joe Stoll, Syracuse University Cartographic Laboratory.

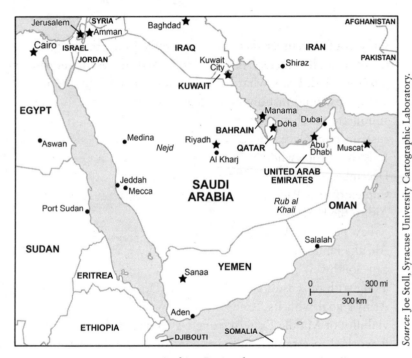

Arabian Peninsula.

# 1

## Double Exposure

*In which we consider the fate of some camels.*

On a cool December day in 2019, I pulled into the parking lot of a small cemetery in Quartzsite, Arizona. As I stepped into the wind, I saw what I was looking for: Hi Jolly's tomb, a stone pyramid just about six feet tall, with a bronze camel silhouette perched on top. The placard, its letters dripping rust since its placement in 1935, read: "The last camp of Hi Jolly. Born somewhere in Syria about 1828, died at Quartzsite December 16, 1902. Came to this country February 10 1856. Cameldriver – Packer – Scout – Over thirty years a Faithful Aid to the U.S. government."

Few people in Arizona know the story of Hi Jolly (aka Hajji Ali, aka Philip Tedro), but he was originally sent to the American Southwest in the 1850s, after the Army picked him up, along with dozens of camels, from the Ottoman Empire. The Army's goal with its "Camel Corps" project was to test the viability of Middle Eastern camels as beasts of burden while it worked to establish military control of the desert Southwest. The US Army had no one in its ranks who knew how to drive, load, or manage the camels, so they imported a cohort of cameleers as well. Most of Hi Jolly's Ottoman companions had lied about their camel expertise to get free passage to America, but he was the only one who actually knew how to handle them. In this way, he came to be seen as a faithful aid to the US government just as the placard claims—ensuring the

**Figures 1.1–1.2.** *Hi Jolly's Last Camp in Quartzsite, Arizona.*

success of the Camel Corps project and advancing the Army's effort to colonize the desert Southwest.

How did a Syrian camel driver end up as a central figure in the American quest to colonize the Arizona desert in the 1800s? What does Hi Jolly's story reveal about the entangled fates of deserts on opposite sides of the globe? What can his forgotten, rusted-over tomb teach us about how this history of American-Arabian connection and empire building has faded into obscurity? As it turns out, Hi Jolly's Quartzsite tomb is as clear a monument as one can find to this little-known American history of arid empire building.

A nineteenth-century army experiment with camels may not seem that relevant to big questions of empire and geopolitics today. But as this book shows, the obscured entanglement of Arizona and Arabia's development offers important lessons about the people, ideas, institutions, and the cultural imaginings of empire: a far-reaching structure of settlement and extraction at work at home and abroad, in the past and still today. In this light, Hi Jolly's tomb is anything but a quirky footnote to American history. It is a place that opens up new perspectives on US settler colonialism, overseas empire, and our colonial present. It is an icon of arid empire.

Like Hi Jolly's tomb, arid empire exists today. To see arid empire, to bring it into focus, we need to examine what I see as the *political lives of deserts*. In the US Southwest, arid empire is partly about the dispossession, expulsion, and extermination of Indigenous communities from these desert lands. But it is also about how American settlers have told—and continue to tell—stories about the "desert" as a place of strength and opportunity, and how these stories are put to work in the name of science, the state, and many other agendas. Even as Arizona's early settlers mastered the skills of colonizing desert, they did not stop there: they took that imperial knowhow back to Arabia, shifting from serving America's empire building "at home" to helping expand its empire overseas.

Arid empire exists today in another sense: in the lives of descendants of empire like myself. Growing up in Tucson, Arizona, in the 1980s and '90s, I was not taught the violent history of Arizona's colonization. Instead, I learned Arizona history from family trips to the iconic places of the "Wild West" —Tombstone and Bisbee and the Old Tucson Studios, where so many cowboy movies had been filmed, and where colonialism was transformed into thrilling tales of Arizona's unruly heroes. These Wild West stories were just a natural part of my childhood home.

Even after I went on to become a geography professor, I never reflected on how it was that I had come to see Arizona as somehow *mine*. I understood the colonial origins of the United States intellectually, but I never directly confronted my personal place in this history and what it meant to be a descendent of white settlers today. It was ultimately my academic studies in the deserts of the Middle East that led me back to deeper questions about Arizona's colonization—where I found myself saddened by the history, as well as my ignorance of arid empire's past *and* present. As I began investigating Hi Jolly's story and the fate of the Middle Eastern camels in the US Southwest, I found that I needed to train myself to see deserts as *political*.

Of course, deserts encompass a vast array of biological, biophysical, and material forces—flora, fauna, human life, sand, water, sun, mineral deposits, and space itself. But people imagine and commodify these resources in remarkable ways, setting them in motion around the world through a range of political networks. In this global circuitry, and in this story of arid empire, the very idea of "desert" itself becomes a resource. Understanding the political lives of deserts is to understand how people tap into this narrative resource, how they breathe life into their stories of the desert, how they put these stories to work through a constellation of desires and beliefs that have accrued to desert landscapes. Camels and all.

\*  \*  \*

The camels and cameleers arrived at Indianola, Texas, on the Gulf of Mexico coast, in 1856. This was their first time in North America, and neither the animals nor their escorts knew whether they would like the continent—but many of the cameleers, if not the camels, suspected they would. The camels had traveled from several spots around the Middle East, including Tunis, Alexandria, Crimea, Malta, and Constantinople. The group of thirty-three pack animals was slowly collected over the course of weeks, making a grand tour of the region by ship. Along the way, one camel ended up getting an itch and was sold off in Constantinople, destined for the butcher's block; another Tunisian camel joined in his fate. The others, however, eventually made their way across the Atlantic aboard the USS *Supply*, a storeship commanded by Lieutenant David D. Porter.[1]

Porter had recently unloaded supplies for US forces in the Mediterranean, when he was given orders to secure his special camel cargo. An 1855 Congressional appropriation footed the $30,000 bill for the mission. It was pushed through by Secretary of War Jefferson Davis. For several years, Davis had been trying to get the appropriation through Congress. He was convinced that camels were the key to unlocking the American West—or rather, the key to *making* it the "American" West. Camels, he and many of his War Department colleagues argued, were vital pack animals in desert settings. Known for their endurance and their unique ability to drink brackish water and store it for long periods of travel, camels were said to be the quintessential necessity for trans-desert transport. Their striking silhouettes are firmly lodged in the Western imagination in images of caravans trekking across the desert sands of Arabia, Africa, and Eurasia.

Having spent time in the desert Southwest during the Mexican-American War, Davis understood the challenges of transport in the region's rail- and roadless landscape. For US state-builders to maintain and strengthen their hold on the region, they needed to increase the presence of central authority, both in terms of government representatives and their visibility. This required supplies. It also required an ability to quickly deploy official representatives, like the men of the US Army, whom Davis oversaw. Advisers suggested that camels might be one way to overcome both challenges in building America's arid empire. Davis was eventually convinced, and argued for the 1855 Congressional appropriation that sent Lieutenant Porter and the storeship *Supply* around the Middle East and North Africa to collect various camel species that might be tested out for Army use in the American West. (The unfortunate camel that developed the itch before landing in America didn't pass muster.)

Most people today can easily picture the shape of the continental US—a bounded entity, with sharp edges at the East and West coasts, and along the land borders with Canada and Mexico.[2] When Hi Jolly and the camels arrived in the mid-1800s, however, the borders recognizable to us today were only just starting to take shape. Within a few short years, from 1846 to 1848, huge swaths of territory were added to the US West. After the Mexican-American War ended in 1848, the United States took possession of the land that today comprises California, Nevada, Utah, Arizona, and parts of neighboring states. In 1853, the Gadsden Purchase added further territory to southern Arizona and New Mexico.[3]

When we imagine any political map, we typically assume that a government is in control of the land within its tidily drawn borders. In this view, the Oregon annexation or the Mexican cession looks like a smooth transfer of power, requiring just a simple revision of lines on paper. Yet the US state was a fuzzy thing in the mid-1800s, and it was not entirely clear where its territorial power began and ended. What the maps of US territorial expansion fail to show is that authorities acting in the name of the American state truly struggled to

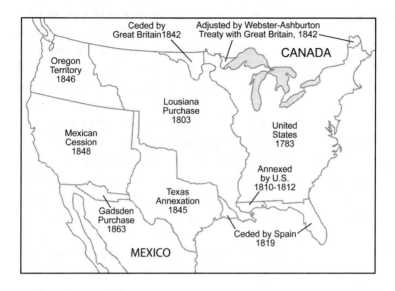

*Figures 1.3–1.4. US territorial expansion.*

gain control of these lands.⁴ This turbulent process belies the image of a neatly bounded territory that American mapmakers wanted to convey in the era of expansion. But the state itself had to be created: it had to be fashioned in people's imaginations, and built into a palpable, material presence. A state can't be made real by cartographers alone.

The US Army's spending on transportation and military post provisions increased drastically between 1845 and 1850 due to the country's sudden westward expansion. The lack of established transportation links to move people and goods through the new Western territories precipitated a tenfold increase in oxen, horses, horseshoes, mules, and mule shoes. These animals also had to be fed, and the Army's outlay for their supplies of hay, grain, and fodder increased from $3.51 per month in 1845 to $10 per month in 1851. The grand total spent on animals for military activities in 1850 was more than twelve times what it was in 1845.⁵

The thirty-three camels brought from the Middle East, Jefferson Davis, then the Secretary of War, imagined, were part of the solution to these challenges—economically and practically expanding American empire into the western reaches of the continent. Compared to the huge sums the Army was spending on animal provisions, the $30,000 Congressional appropriation seemed negligible. If successful, the camel experiment could mean significant cost savings even in terms of feed alone—the animals would not require provisions but could be sustained by simply browsing on any passing vegetation in the desert.

Notable among the camels' boosters was George Perkins Marsh, who would later be called America's first environmentalist. In an influential Smithsonian Institute speech in 1854, he waxed poetic about the camel, noting that "by discovering the hidden wells of the waste and the islands of verdure that surround them," the camel "has made permanently habitable vast regions not otherwise penetrable by man."[6] But Marsh wasn't just a naturalist. He became familiar with the camel during his time as a US envoy in the Ottoman Empire from 1850 to 1853. Drawing from his observations of local Arab and Bedouin uses of the dromedary camel in transport and in battle, as well as by the French and British agents of empire in the region, he felt confident that the US Army could reap many of the same benefits. The goal, of course, was not natural science but making the desert "permanently habitable."

For Marsh, the camel needed to be understood from two angles: as a "beast of burden" and as an "animal of war." As all contemporary writers emphasized, the camel could easily surpass all other animals in bearing heavy loads. Transporting munitions and military stores was thus one obvious benefit of using camels, Marsh noted.[7] Less obvious was its potential in combat. Reflecting on the French imperial officers' ambivalence toward the camel's usefulness in war, he came to the animal's defense for its potential in the American West, boldly arguing:

The prejudices of the officers and men against the use of this awkward and ungraceful animal in the regular service have proved very difficult to overcome. [...] It is, however, proved that the use of the dromedary contributes in a most important degree to the economy, the celerity, and the efficiency of military movements in desert regions; and I cannot doubt that it would prove a most powerful auxiliary in all measures tending to keep in check the hostile Indians on the frontier, as well as in maintaining the military and postal communication between our Pacific territory and the east. There are few more imposing spectacles than a body of armed men advancing under the quick pace of the trained dromedary; and this sight, with the ability of the animal to climb ascents impracticable to horses, and thus to transport mountain howitzers, light artillery, stores, and other military materiel into the heart of the mountains, would strike with a salutary terror the Comanches, Lipans, and other savage tribes upon our borders.[8]

In throwing his support behind the camel, Marsh was of one mind with Jefferson Davis. For both men, advocating for the camel's introduction to the desert Southwest was about strategically reducing the challenges of territorial control to one of physical geography and the natural world. These men were not interested in *why* Indigenous communities were so fiercely resisting US expansion, but rather *how* to stop that resistance. Colonialism was taken for granted as a noble cause—call it "manifest destiny"—and the camel merely an ally in that civilizing quest.

The US colonization of North America was built on the idea that land and resources are wealth. In this imperial vision, nature was a wellspring of opportunity to be tapped by human ingenuity or simple persistence. As America's borders moved west, empire thus unspooled through farming and homesteading as much as through military conquest. The natural features of the arid West confounded European settlers, however. The unfamiliar desert ecology and climate meant that they could not easily deploy their trusted models of farming, animal husbandry, and commerce in places with limited access to water, high and variable temperatures, different soil compositions, and unique wildlife types and distributions. To address this challenge, empire builders in nineteenth-century America took Middle Eastern deserts as a key source of inspiration. Jefferson Davis's camels were one of the earliest examples of how this worked.

For American settlers, the challenge was not just surviving in this new environment but to transform their mere presence into something solid resembling "state power." Taming the farthest reaches of the North American continent was about much more than mere survival. Settlers were also setting out to transform the land into a *homeland*. Of course, the "American" West was already someone else's homeland. Contrary to popular American myths purveyed by advocates of US expansion in the 1800s (and still today), the West was not a "virgin land."[9] It was and continues to be the home of diverse Indigenous communities, from the Diné to the Apache, Zuni, Pima.

The desert landscape was not "foreign" for these communities; it was simply home. As with any home, the desert was fraught with challenges for its residents, but it was not a place to be "conquered." Nor was it a place approached with the profit-centered logic of extraction. White settlers, by contrast, were recruited to the Southwest with promises of the great wealth that could be reaped from capitalist enterprises like commercial farming or mining, or perhaps great power from careers in the military and territorial administration. In this way, the dominant settler story about the desert was that it could be a natural *and* national "resource" to be exploited. But as Diné geographer Andrew Curley has succinctly put it, "*Resources* is just another word for colonialism."[10]

For most Indigenous residents, the desert was a place of community and life, a place to be sustained rather than exploited for capitalist profiteering. But this way of knowing and relating to the desert did not align with the colonial logic of extraction, so settlers actively worked to remove Native residents just as they had done elsewhere in North America. Building arid empire in the US West was in part about displacing these people through genocide and war, but it was also about displacing their knowledge and ways of relating to the land.[11] Since Anglo-European settlers did not arrive in the arid West with an understanding of the desert themselves, they drew on other sources of desert knowhow to fulfill their dreams of conquering the dry landscape of the Southwest.

American travel writers, explorers, scientists, and government officials had long described the arid West as a local version of the Middle Eastern and North African desert—an

"American Zahara" or a Biblical Orient with spiritual and physical power equal to the Old World deserts that populated the Judeo-Christian imaginations of American settlers.[12] These authors harnessed the "Sahara" trope, Catrin Gersdorf argues, "to deactivate the existential anxieties of the pioneers and to alleviate some of their visceral reactions to the American West's aridity, recasting it as a quasi-Oriental space containing yet unidentified but extremely valuable historical and cultural riches."[13] Nineteenth-century authors' constant references to the Sahara and other Biblical landscapes helped the predominantly Christian settlers imagine the newly American desert lands as a "domestic" Orient and, in this way, somehow familiar.

Desert landscapes terrified many would-be settlers in the arid West, but so did the Indigenous residents, with whom the US Army waged overt war into the early 1900s. Displacing the people from the land was one thing, but redefining their social and cultural association with the desert was a different matter. Here again, the camel proved useful. This is vividly illustrated when the Army finally collected enough camels in Texas to run its first Camel Corps trial to assess the animals' endurance and suitability for military purposes. The Army's man in charge, General Edward Fitzgerald Beale, brought Hi Jolly, his fellow cameleers, and a large camel caravan together to travel from Texas to California beginning in September 1857.[14] When the expedition stopped in Los Angeles in January 1858, the *San Francisco Evening Bulletin* described the scene with dramatized gusto:

> General Beale and about fourteen camels stalked into town last Friday week and gave our streets quite an Oriental aspect. It looked oddly enough to see outside of a menagerie, a herd of huge, ungainly awkward but docile animals move about in our midst with people riding them like horses and bringing up weird and far-off associations to the Eastern traveler, whether by book or otherwise of the land of the mosque, crescent or turban, of

the pilgrim mufti and dervish with visions of the great shrines
of the world, Mecca and Jerusalem, and the toiling throngs
that have for centuries wended thither, of the burning sands of
Arabia and Sahara where the desert is boundless as the ocean
and the camel is the ship thereof.[15]

This account actively rewrites the then-dominant imaginary of
US West as the domain of hostile Native Americans, enlisting
the camel to transform it into a whimsical vision of the Old
World in the New. No longer the home of "savage tribes," the
desert was instead cast as a miniature Holy Land. Colonization was made friendlier by conceiving of it as a pilgrimage,
an act of return. By directly linking to the familiar visions of
Middle Eastern deserts that fill the Bible, the American deserts
could start to feel more familiar too. In this way, the territories
annexed in the mid-1800s could begin to be imagined as an
individual settler's home, and the arid empire as part of the
homeland. For what else is home but familiar?

General Beale was an avid supporter of the Camel Corps
and he used the animals for diverse projects through 1861.
However, the lack of funding and governmental support led
the Army to scrap the effort by the time the Civil War broke
out.[16] The camels were dispersed to the winds, and so too
were the cameleers, Hi Jolly included. For his part, he must
have found something familiar in the Arizona desert too, for
he made Arizona his home. He married a Tucson woman,
Gertrude, and when they eventually separated—"Cameldriver –
Packer – Scout" that he was—Hi Jolly moved to the more
sparsely populated area of Quartzsite till the end of his days.
    When I visited in 2019, I found that the town is still a place
that attracts eccentrics—hippie geode hunters and "off-the-
land" white nationalists alike. ATVs of all shapes and sizes
buzz people in and out of town: the surrounding desert is
filled with their RVs, haphazardly strewn over the flat and

dusty land. It was hard to imagine the ATVs replaced with Hi Jolly astride a hulking camel, traversing the rocky terrain. But in many ways, he was their direct predecessor: a transplant from another land who helped realize the colonial vision in the desert. If, as his "last camp" memorial plaque suggests, he was a "faithful aid to the U.S. government," then he was also an agent of empire, even if an unwitting one.

Thinking about Hi Jolly forced me to ask if I am an unconscious agent of empire as well, a player in the drama of arid empire. From a young age, my brother and I consumed and reenacted the Wild West in everything from picture books to film to childhood games of Cowboys and Indians. We would dutifully don our cowboy and cowgirl attire for Tucson's annual February rodeo, hayrides and birthday parties, and anything else that demanded western flair. Of course our lives didn't remotely resemble the Wild West. But when we were growing up, the Sonoran desert surrounding Tucson had become the most iconic landscape representing the Wild West in English-language film and television—and we were tremendously proud of it. Seeing our familiar desert on screen, with its towering saguaro silhouettes dotting sweeping valleys and rugged cliffs, we reveled in being able to call Arizona home. We were proud to join the ranks of the "gunfighter nation"[17] that valiantly (we thought) brought this land under control.

But as Lakota scholar and activist Nick Estes recently remarked in an interview, "When you say the 'Wild West,' you're talking about *genocide*." It was "at the end of a gun and a bayonet," that US democracy was built.[18] Estes is right, of course. But my cowgirl upbringing was not only built at the altar of violence sanitized and sanctified. It was also built through positive associations with the land. I would spend hours roaming the desert outside my house, collecting cactus and plant specimens and building forts in the thick mesquite underbrush. I learned the textures of the desert flora and its rocky terrain. I understood the animals and their movements

**Figures 1.5–1.6.** *The author and her brother in 1989 and 1990.*

well. I came to know the feel and flavor of the Sonoran desert and I reveled in it too.

As I started to chase Hi Jolly and the camels through this desert's history, I was forced to admit that my love for Arizona's landscapes never was, and never could be, innocent. Of course, I couldn't call any other soil or mountains or valleys "home." I was born and raised in this place. Ultimately, though, I was raised on myth. I was born into the American structure of settler colonialism that cast me as an actor in the theater of much longer and larger debates about whose "native soil" Arizona really was. But the power of arid empire, I came to realize, rested in how it could make these myths and structures invisible.

Cowboy kitsch and Hollywood-ready landscapes helped me to experience Arizona history as a guilt-free space of fantasy, completely divorced from political questions about how Arizona became part of the United States, and how someone like me came to call it home. I cannot blame anyone for my happy childhood as a cowgirl. But by learning to apply the retrospective lens of arid empire, as Hi Jolly's tomb begs us to do, I have come to understand the colonial structure that I was born into. My early romance with the desert is not guilt-free. It is an *achievement*. It is the result of the calculated effort of generations of settlers—and their camels, horses, and mules— who created the conditions for me to call Arizona home and to personally live out their vision of civilization in the desert. As a way of seeing, arid empire forces me—forces us—to ask how this colonial project was built on fictional stories about the desert, and on real ones too.

It took me leaving Arizona to actually see arid empire and my own place in it. As a scholar, I have traveled to many overseas deserts, from the vast steppes of Central Asia to the dunes of Egypt and the Arabian Peninsula. In learning about all these other places, I became acquainted with the idiosyncrasies of their deserts and desert cultures. I ended up riding camels, drinking camel's milk, visiting camel markets, eating camel burgers, and watching camels with little Japanese robot jockeys train for high-stakes races. I even bought extra-luxury camel milk soap. But I never questioned whether the camel "belonged" in these places. That they did was simply obvious fact.

One day in 2014, I found myself watching television in a hotel in Qatar. The set was tuned to Al Jazeera, and they were showing a short documentary about the camel. It had the grand, sweeping language of any hagiographic account of an animal heralded as a national emblem. I was already intimately familiar with such descriptions of camels in the Arabian Peninsula: just like the Qatari (or Emirati or Saudi) nation, the camel was valiant, resilient, tenacious, a marvel to behold! The well-scripted nationalist formula took an unexpected turn, however, when the host started talking about how Arabian camels had been transported overseas to Australia and the United States long ago. Feral camels, I learned, still roam (and ravage) the Australian outback, though they have since disappeared from the US.[19] How curious, I thought, before turning to other things.

Four years later, I found myself recalling the American and Australian camels while reflecting on the curious connections between different deserts of the world. From seeming happenstance, I stumbled into a rich but largely ignored history of exchanges between Arizona and the Arabian Peninsula. The fates of these two desert places have been entangled for at least 150 years. Unlike some histories of empire, however, these connections are not obvious. They are hidden from public view in a way that formal colonialism, like that of Spain in Latin America or Britain in India, isn't.

Understanding arid empire was, for me, an intimate journey because I discovered that this invisibility was a privilege that I inherited as a descendant of white American settlement in

Arizona. I never had to grapple with the grief and generational trauma of Indigenous peoples dispossessed from this land; instead, my whiteness hid the history of colonization from me. Despite this, the Arizona desert still led me to its colonial history, for my personal experience in the Arizona desert—my love for it, perhaps—helped me also see its contours in the geographies of the Arabian Peninsula. As I came to specialize in Arab Gulf studies, I moved through its intellectual spaces without being aware—without *having* to be aware—that I was actually one in a long line of white researchers and arid lands experts from Arizona who had profited from their desert familiarity long before me.

And it was this personal and intellectual journey that led me to Quartzsite, staring at the camel-topped tomb of Hi Jolly that afternoon in December 2019. I had just come from visiting a Saudi-owned farm thirty minutes east, where alfalfa was being grown as fodder for that country's massive dairy industry. And I was just about to visit some palm orchards that helped start the US date industry that began in the late 1800s with some varieties imported from the Arabian Peninsula. These curious connections were hard enough to map, let alone to make sense of intellectually. Eventually, it was another camel encounter that helped me better understand the scope of this arid empire stretching from Arizona to the Arabian Peninsula.

Almost sixty years before I first set foot in Saudi Arabia as a young geography professor, a predecessor of mine in Syracuse University's Geography Department visited too. George Babcock Cressey joined the university in 1931 and presided over the Geography Department as chair for decades. Born in Ohio in 1896, Cressey was a prolific traveler. He spent a great deal of his early life in China and got his start teaching at the University of Shanghai in the 1920s. Cressey was a prolific scholar and a passionate photographer, and after he settled in Syracuse, he never gave up his frequent international travels.

When he was a Fulbright Scholar in Iraq in the 1950s, Cressey wanted to expand his research on deserts to include the Arabian Peninsula. So he contacted the (then) American oil company Aramco and the company gamely facilitated his travels, which he documented in a series of beautiful color slide photographs. Going through these in Syracuse's Special Collections, one image from the Saudi heartland, the Nejd, immediately captivated me—and continued to haunt me long afterward. Merely labeled "Camel/Coke Double Exposure," the slide shows a lone camel in the sand dunes transposed over a road sign advertising Coca-Cola along a dusty desert road.

The "Camel/Coke" double exposure image opened up a torrent of questions for me, which were not so much about Cressey as about myself. If Cressey had been interested in exactly the same spot in central Saudi Arabia that I now was, but decades before, could I be anything more than a successor to his old-fashioned geography? Was I bound to tread the same path that Western geographers studying deserts had long

*Source:* George Cressey Papers, University Archives, Special Collections Research Center, Syracuse University Libraries *(digitally altered for clarity, with permission).*

*Figure 1.7. "Camel/Coke double exposure," slide photograph from SU professor's visit to Saudi Arabia in the 1950s.*

established—traveling to foreign lands to extract knowledge about deserts and fashion themselves as arid lands "experts"? Were my questions today actually any different from the extractivist knowledge economy that shaped how geographers approached desert lands in Cressey's time?

Cressey's photograph brought arid empire into focus in a new way for me, forcing me to reflect on the way that images like the camel, the desolate dune backdrop, and the consumerist Coke icon are all part of the symbolic repertoire that arid lands experts used to fashion American understandings of the Arabian Peninsula. I too have wandered through the Arabian Peninsula to understand its cultural, political, and physical geography. I too have photographed camels and Western road signs. I too have stood as an American in these deserts trying to make sense of it. In some ways, I can only understand the Arabian Peninsula by thinking about Arizona: a double exposure.

The double exposure is no error. It truly is a camel of the Saudi desert affixed to the commercial forces of America: Coke, roads, sand, and all. To get to this point—that a US geographer should find himself capturing these images with the help of an oil company that would transform the Arabian Peninsula and global geopolitics writ large—Saudi and American leaders, technocrats, farmers, scientists, and countless others needed to align their interests through their stories of commonality and their entangled fates of arid empire. Material realities like water, money, sunshine, machinery, and men are needed to tell these stories. And so is the ability to look at past and present together, and to see Cressey's "Camel/Coke" double exposure not as an error, but just like Hi Jolly's tomb in Quartzsite, as an icon of arid empire.

While my first trips to the Middle East were shaped by an acute awareness of US imperialism in the region, my grasp on American empire was nonetheless narrow. I knew about the oil and military relations that defined US influence in the Arabian

Peninsula, but I wasn't thinking of imperialism running through the networks I consider in this book: agriculture, science and arid lands expertise, and experiments with technomodernist futures in the desert. And crucially, my awareness of American empire in the Middle East never included the history of how it had been built on the foundations of the United States' *domestic* empire in the desert Southwest. It was only when I started to reflect on the connections between Arizona and the Arabian Peninsula that I came to see how arid empire was a joint project—that these imperialisms built one another. In the "Camel/Coke" image is a way to see double, across time and space, and to *be* double too: to keep that multiplicity and tension in focus without trying to clear the way for a singular vision.

This book sets out to understand the history of arid empire binding Arizona and Arabia in double exposure—refracted not just across time and space, but also bodies and lives. Reflecting on my own place in this history, I cannot escape the role of how American empire has come to structure politics in the Arabian Peninsula and globally over the past century. I cannot escape the brutal reality of territorial dispossession that *is* the United States and my "home state" of Arizona. But with a dose of curiosity and openness to surprise, I can refuse arid empire's politics of invisibility and find the fissures that might allow a new politics of visibility to peek through. By learning to see double, to *see* arid empire, I need not be the little cowgirl cast as an actor in someone else's colonial theater. I have more choices than being ventriloquized or silenced: I can unravel my own expectations of history, of my own fantasies of good and evil and, just maybe, know the desert differently. Jefferson Davis and his camels be damned.

# 2

## Dates

*In which we follow the early days of America's arid empire through the promiscuous travels of the Arabian date palm, first planted in Arizona in the 1890s and later repackaged as a settler's route to that most valuable of commodities, arid lands agriculture "expertise."*

The Arabian Peninsula, like other parts of the Middle East and North Africa, has a deep cultural connection to dates and date palms, and for Oman in particular, much of the country's economy, prestige, and lifeways have centered around date production. Travel through the country's rural villages and you will see that settlements invariably have individual- and community-managed farms, and that each community's geography is determined by the world-renowned Omani *aflaj* channels that distribute spring water to the palm orchards. Omanis have a centuries-old tradition of preparing dates in as many different forms as possible—whole, in jams, in syrups. Palm fronds and fibers are used to make everything from roofs to rope to rugs. Dates were one of the most important exports of the country throughout the nineteenth century, and their sale both enriched local merchants and extended the international influence of the sultanate.

However, in 2018, the Omani government signed a $3.9 million deal with the University of Arizona to help Oman develop its date industry by establishing a new date palm research laboratory outside of Muscat.[1] The project was supported by the Omani government's "Million Date Palm Plantation Project," which began in 2009 under the direction of the late Sultan of Oman, Qaboos bin Said al Said. It remains a government-sponsored initiative based in the Diwan of the Royal Court with the stated aim of "establishing a modern date palm sector in the sultanate."[2] The project is part of the country's broader economic diversification efforts, and the hope is that Oman can develop a commercial base for date production, since the country's agriculture is today dominated by small plots and privately run farms. Indeed, Oman has not had large-scale date production since commercial exports collapsed in the early 1900s.

Oman's neighbors, Saudi Arabia and the United Arab Emirates, by contrast, have steadily developed large commercial date operations. Given their lack of domestic infrastructure, Omani producers often ship their dates to these neighbors for packing and distribution. To the outrage of many Omanis, *their* dates are thus rebranded as Saudi or Emirati, and resold at a much higher price. This situation is what the Million Date Palm initiative was designed to change; it now sponsors twelve commercial farms across the country and will soon open Oman's first large-scale date packing facility.

The $3.9 million that the grant paid out to the University of Arizona purchased the Americans' scientific expertise in setting up the state-of-the-art Central Date Palm Laboratory at a farm in Sumail—a rural locale about a forty-five-minute drive from Muscat, Oman. The lab includes facilities for tissue culturing and research on pests, disease, and the genetic composition of date varieties for commercial production. Though UA staff set up the lab, the grant stipulated that the entire project would then transfer to Omani scientists over a three-year period.

The date palm laboratory project was, for the University of Arizona, a financial opportunity: the contract represented a boon for university coffers. It also bolstered the institution's

*Source*: Author, January 2020.

*Figure 2.1. View of the Million Date Palms farm in Sumail, Oman. The UA-supported Central Date Palm Laboratory under development is visible in the background.*

narrative of collaboration between the University of Arizona and the greater Middle East, where some of UA's most generous institutional donors hail from. As Brent White, then UA's vice provost for global affairs and dean of global campuses, explained after the 2018 signing ceremony for the date lab: "The University of Arizona has a longstanding relationship with our valued partners in the Middle East, particularly in the Gulf states. This project will enhance these relationships and, more importantly, spur scientific discovery that will positively impact Oman and people worldwide."[3]

The flowery language of relationships built on "scientific discovery" aside, there are two questions here: given Oman's intimate history with dates, why was the University of Arizona, of all places, chosen for this project? And how is it that US researchers could claim expertise in date palm agriculture when if anyone can claim to be the preeminent authority on anything date-related, it should be the Omanis themselves?

These questions have surface answers, primarily related to alumni networks and the specifics of governmental funding rules in Oman, but they become even more intriguing when we look at the university's deeper history with date palms. Date-related exchanges between UA and the Middle East began in the 1890s, when the University of Arizona imported its first date palm varieties from the Arabian Peninsula, Omani ones included. The trees were to be tested at the university's brand-new Agriculture Experiment Station, a laboratory that was instrumental to the university's founding and that helped the institution position itself as a leader in arid lands agriculture.

In other words, the University of Arizona's expertise in date palm agriculture that the Omani government purchased in 2018 came from … Oman, and its neighbors. This history of date palm knowledge exchanged and bought and sold shows how "expertise" in arid land agriculture—more even than the date palm itself—was the most valuable commodity in the creation of arid empire. Buying and selling knowledge about dates not only linked Arizona and Arabia together scientifically and institutionally, but also produced a resource of sorts—expertise —that could be extracted, sought after, controlled.

For many years, the University of Arizona existed on paper only. Arizona's colonial leaders first considered establishing a university shortly after Arizona was recognized as a US territory by Congress in December 1863, but the project floundered for decades. The Territorial Legislature finally authorized a university for development in Tucson in 1885 and created a Board of Regents. The legislature put forward some of the funds needed to build the university's first structures, but left the regents to find the rest of the money to cover construction fees on their own, as well as other operating expenses. In 1887, the board eventually secured a land donation and the ground for the campus was broken. The money quickly ran out, and two years later, the first campus building remained unfinished.

In the summer of 1889, however, the UA board learned it could access funding from the Hatch Act of 1887, a supplement to the 1862 Morrill Act, also known as the Land-Grant College Act. The Hatch Act offered grants of $15,000 a year to land grant colleges in order to build and operate agricultural experiment stations. The regents saw the Hatch Act as their chance to get funding to finish the university's first buildings, so they hurriedly concocted a plan for an Experiment Station and filed for federal funding. Despite the fact that the station existed on paper only and was "run" by the only UA regent with a college degree (the lawyer Selim Franklin), the regents' application was successful. The money started flowing several months later, in June 1890. The university's first building, Old Main, was finished the following year, just in time for UA's first students to arrive in October 1891.

The Morrill Act of 1862, along with the 1887 Hatch Act and a second Morrill Act passed in 1890, served as the legislative basis for the "land grant" system designed to support colleges specializing in "agriculture and the mechanic arts." Through the Morrill Act, designated land grant institutions in each US state were given huge tracts of federally controlled land to help raise their initial endowments—much of it taken dubiously or illegally from Native Americans in the newly claimed American West. Most universities were eager to turn a profit, so they quickly sold off the granted land in lucrative parcels (only a handful still control these parcels today).[4] In this way, the American education system became an important tool for westward expansion and Indigenous displacement.

So too did agriculture. Over the course of the 1800s, American colonialism was infused with the ideals of Jeffersonian agrarianism, especially as agrarian populist movements became increasingly influential in national policymaking. Much the same as American agricultural idealism today, the hero in the nineteenth century's agrarian populist utopia was the white farmer. Hardy and determined sower of civilization that he was imagined to be, the farmer just needed land to ignite his entrepreneurial spirit. By granting the farmer-hero access to

"unused" or "underused" public land—so rich! so fertile!—
the agrarian empire builders saw him as the key to rapidly
transforming and "civilizing" the farthest reaches of the continent. Advocates of this mission shared the same objectives of
displacing Indigenous claims to the land that Jefferson Davis
and his camel-loving allies did. They just approached it with
a different toolkit.

This romantic vision was appealing to many colonial deci-
sionmakers in Washington, DC, and other Eastern power
centers in the mid- to late 1800s. Agrarian interests had started
to become a powerful force in national politics, and advocates
used that influence to shape federal policy.[5] There were endless
legislative battles about how best to plant this fictional farmer
in the land, but one favored tactic to territorialize American
control of the West was to distribute "public" land, usually illegally seized from Native communities.[6] A flurry of programs to
grant land to settlers and their institutions in the West included
the two Morrill Acts and the Hatch Act.

Beyond these, multiple iterations of the 1862 Homestead Act
and the 1877 Desert Lands Act aimed to encourage farmers
to move to the region not long after the camels had made
their noble but short-lived treks across the desert. Whereas the
Homestead Act opened up "unclaimed" public lands to homestead farmers west of the Mississippi, the Desert Lands Act was
specifically designed to attract homesteaders to irrigate and
cultivate arid and semiarid lands. Collectively, U.S. federal land
distribution helped wrest control from Indigenous communities
and sow its imperial seeds: the white settler farmers themselves.

At this time, agriculturalists were dealing with major challenges in the sphere of higher education—namely, that most
of the students they wanted to mold into noble settler-farmers
did not actually need the instruction land grant colleges were
offering. In some cases, the students had grown up farming
and had been learning the trade their entire lives; in others,
these young boys would leave farming behind entirely after a

college education gave them ideas about alternative careers. Legislators and agrarian advocates hotly debated the problem, but everyone agreed that land grant colleges needed to scrap the common programs of sending students to work on "model farms" and instead develop a more "scientific" approach to agricultural education. That is, colleges needed to produce not just farmers but expertise.

By the late 1800s, colleges had started to develop "agricultural experiment stations," where professional researchers would serve as liaisons for the farming community. They would help research the most pressing problems of local farmers but, crucially, they would do so without co-opting the farming communities' youth by bringing them into the college system as students. This approach seemed to be a promising solution; and thus the Hatch Act was born. By supporting the opening and maintenance of experiment stations, the act promised to help the land-grant colleges to fulfill their broader mission of serving local communities by bringing them science-based knowledge—that imagined special offering of an institution of higher education.

The Morrill and Hatch Acts were, at one level, about supporting the development of higher education, but they were ultimately part of a much larger scheme of land distribution and territorial control throughout the still-expanding United States.[7] Given this situation then, when the University of Arizona's Board of Regents saw a chance to cash in on the Hatch Act money in 1889 by submitting an application for its nonexistent "Agricultural Experiment Station," they found a receptive audience in the federal government and its colonial agents. Of course, the Experiment Station couldn't remain a fiction for long.

The first order of business for creating the UA Agricultural Experiment Station (AES) was to hire a director to replace the fictitious leader designated in the original application, Selim

Franklin. Frank A. Gulley, who had previously served as Texas A&M's Experiment Station director, was hired in 1890 as the University of Arizona's first professor. At Arizona, he assumed the role of Dean of the College of Agriculture and became the first Director of the AES.[8]

In the first AES news bulletin, issued in December 1890, Gulley explained that he wanted the Experiment Station's work to be "of the greatest practical value to the residents of the Territory."[9] Implicit but unstated in this declaration is the fact that the AES was not aimed at supporting all Arizona residents: it was firstly about supporting white settlers of the territory, and secondly about supporting commercial farming rather than subsistence agriculture. But since Gulley was an outsider who had just arrived from Texas, he had to do some legwork to make a credible claim that he knew what was of "greatest practical value" to Arizona.

In the year before the University of Arizona officially opened in October 1891, Gulley took up this task and set out to tour the Territory and learn about how best to promote the interests of commercial farmers in Arizona. The members of the farming community convinced him of their strong interest in fruit production, which had already become a focus of agricultural boosterism in Arizona some years before. Gulley's initial plan for the station's work dutifully reproduced the farmers' enthusiasm for fruit, tinged with optimism that it would become one of Arizona's "leading industries."[10]

From the perspective of "modern science," which the university and other scientists in the late 1800s and early 1900s were trying to advance in Arizona and other parts of America's new arid empire, the ultimate goal was to transform the desert into a blossoming paradise for farming. Oriented toward commercial agriculture rather than the subsistence or small-scale farming that Indigenous tribes had long practiced in the area, this reimagined desert was to be brought in line, aesthetically and commercially, with Western and capitalist ideals. That is,

# Southern Arizona's · FRUIT LANDS.

## Happy Homes, Health and Wealth.

ARIZONA is divided by the thirty-fourth parallel of north latitude into two climatic zones, each distinct from the other. On the elevated plateau of Northern Arizona, between the southern boundary of Utah and the thirty-fourth parallel, four thousand to six thousand feet above the level of the sea, the temperature ranges during the year from 90° to 10° above zero. South of this region the altitude is from two thousand to four thousand feet less and the climate is much warmer.

It is not the purpose of this pamphlet to speak of northern Arizona—its delightful and invigorating climate, its immense forests of timber, its extensive coal measures, its marvelous mines of gold, silver and copper, its unexcelled grazing lands, its valleys which grow in endless profusion all kinds of cereals, vegetables and the hardier fruits, its fertile soil equal in productive capacity to that of any portion of the world,—all these deserve and will receive attention in a future article.

Our subject at present will be Southern Arizona and its remarkable adaptability to fruit growing.

**Figure 2.2.** *Introduction to the 1887 publication of Phoenix Commissioner of Immigration, Cameron H. King,* The Citrus and Fruit Belt of Southern Arizona.

colonized land was to be "civilized" by bringing it under commercial cultivation.[11]

For his part, Gulley was eager to show that the Territory's new university was committed to being an ally of local farmers, whose ability to cultivate desert land was at the heart of America's new arid empire. His early efforts to develop the AES are emblematic of the kind of relationship between higher education and the farming community that colonial planners wanted to spark with the Morrill and Hatch Acts. In the mid- and late 1800s, lawmakers and expansionist politicians in Washington were captivated by the potential of harnessing science and agricultural education to strengthen US control of its newly acquired territories. This was true across the country, but if getting white settlers to stay in the new lands was key to establishing control of the West, a special kind of desert farming expertise was apparently needed to help would-be farmers. This was an effort that AES was eager to sign on to.

For a brief moment, it seems that Gulley considered another audience for the AES to target: Native Americans. In July 1891, he wrote to the US assistant secretary of agriculture, Edwin Willits, to ask for his support in an AES initiative to collaborate with the Office of Indian Affairs on "co-operative work in the interest of the Indians." Gulley explained:

> There are two reasons why we desire to take up this work: First, we want to commit the University in its organization to the education of the Indians as well as the white people of the Territory, and while the ordinary Indian schools are well enough in their way, we believe some method of setting the Indians to work and leading them to earn money and increase their wants, particularly a desire to live like human beings is the only practicable plan by which any permanent good may be secured.
>
> To educate the young Indians, boys or girls and then send them back to the Reservation may be satisfactory to those well meaning people of the east who know nothing of the Indians or of the way in which they live on the Reservations, but the effect on the Indians themselves is demoralizing. We believe we can form a nucleus of industrious Indians and provide a plan whereby some of the boys and girls from the schools will be afforded an opportunity to grow up into good citizens it is true, but under different influences and surroundings.[12]

In addition to the blatant racism masquerading as benevolence, Gulley's letter hints at a more sinister motive for removing Indigenous youth from the reservations to "educate" them—fitting into a wider trend of settler colonial dispossession through Native boarding schools, or what David Adams has referred to as "education for extinction."[13]

A glimpse of this is seen in the second reason that Gulley

gave Willits for proposing the cooperative work with the Office of Indian Affairs—that the AES wanted "to demonstrate on a considerable scale what may be done in irrigation through pumping water." He explained that his staff wanted to experiment with new pumping technologies to see if they could improve fruit production. "We would like to throw some light on this question," he wrote, "and the Pima Reservation lying right in what is rapidly becoming a great fruit section is a most desirable place to establish this object lesson."[14] That is, Pima reservation lands stood in the way of his noble scientific enterprise. Gulley might have had an interest in appropriating Indigenous reservation lands, but it is impossible to know because his proposal apparently failed; the AES archives have no additional record of this project or any other efforts to include Indigenous communities in its work for decades. Yet Gulley's vision of using the AES to help "civilize" Arizona's Native Americans is suggestive of how the university's agricultural experts saw themselves as helping realize an ideal of bringing civilization to the frontier.

Whether patronizing or violent, the civilizing ideal articulated by Gulley has remained a constant theme over many decades of the university's history. In 1960, the UA president, Richard Harvill, showered Douglas Martin's overtly racist history of the university's founding, *Lamp in the Desert*, with praise, writing in the foreword that the journalism professor had "told this story dramatically and with delightful touches of humor."[15] And in 2019, another UA president, Robert Robbins, provoked outrage after using racist language and references in a meeting with a group of Native students, sparking a wider debate about pervasive anti-Indigenous racism on campus. Long after Gulley penned his letter to Washington bureaucrats, Native students and faculty continue to feel that the university serves white settlers as the primary community.[16] With no small dose of foreboding, Gulley's letter shows how men like him and institutions like the University of Arizona

33

*Figure 2.3. University of Arizona Board of Regents letterhead, 1890.*

were to become leaders in the country's new arid empire. In fact, the first official letterhead of university's Board of Regents also carried a strong whiff of foreboding in its bold assertion: "Knowledge is power."

The University of Arizona was just one part of a larger structure of colonial state-making that reshaped the racial geography of the newly American West. A host of US public and private institutions, laws, and intimate interactions worked together to build a majority white citizenry as the country expanded its borders in the 1800s. The racial composition of what is now Arizona was an issue even before it was incorporated into the territorial bounds of the United States. As Paul Frymer explains, race was at the center of how settlement and territorial incorporation was viewed from Washington, with Congressmen and the federal government frequently seeking to "manufacture racially specific outcomes—namely, the establishment of a white demographic stronghold."[17]

Territorial acquisitions that might tip the balance to include large numbers of non-white residents were approached with suspicion. This was evident in the early debates about the lands encompassing contemporary Arizona, California, Nevada, and

Utah, which were added to the United States following the Mexican-American War in 1848. Nicholas P. Trist, President Polk's diplomat sent to negotiate the Treaty of Guadalupe Hidalgo that resulted in this land cession, wrote to DC that "it is not our interest to acquire a territory containing much population, especially if the latter be, as is the case in northern Mexico, of a mixed colored race," and that the population was "too much to take. The population is mostly dark as our mulattoes, and is nominally free, and would be actually so under our government."[18] As Frymer shows, the border negotiations in 1848 thus centered on how to maximize territory and minimize people—ultimately acquiring only 1 percent of the Mexican population.[19]

The racial bigotry that ran through early American expansionism never disappeared; it simply shape-shifted. This meant that even after Arizona became a territory, advocates of statehood knew that having a large white population was key to gaining this status and that they would have to work hard to fight the perception among Washington lawmakers that the territory was home to too many "non-white" residents.[20] Many Arizona boosters were true believers in the United States' foundational myth of white supremacy and "upbuilding"—a contemporary notion of racial "improvement" (i.e., whitening the population).[21] Practically and materially, Arizona's upbuilders operationalized that vision in diverse ways as they found openings to realize their own ambitions for the region through the continent's rapidly changing racial landscape. Agricultural development was among the foremost of these opportunistic openings.

Ensuring the success of settlers was no easy feat in the desert, which most Americans still understood to be foreign and dangerous in the 1800s. To help them adapt and thus tighten their grip on the land, Arizona leaders immediately saw an opportunity to position the Territory's university as an agricultural laboratory. The institution as a whole could help transform the desert "wasteland" into productive land for would-be white settlers from the East. The desert-as-laboratory became an imaginary space—one that can be discerned, dissected, and distinguished from other spaces for the scientific gaze. This desert laboratory was not just for science in the traditional sense, but also a project in social engineering, whereby Anglo-American ideas of "civilization" were to be tested out in geographic settings perceived as starkly different from previous zones of expansion.

This is where arid empire needed modern science. The innovations of modern technology, waterworks, and scientific expertise could be put to work in taming the desert. The fact that groups like the Pima, Gila, Diné and Maricopa all had sophisticated agricultural systems prior to colonization was simply erased from the celebrated stories of "modernizing" Arizona agriculture. Instead, the desert-as-laboratory needed to be imagined as a smooth, emptied space, detached from the messy complexities of politics, greed, and Indigenous erasures that were the necessary conditions for Arizona's takeover. William Smythe's framing of the desert West in his 1900 book *The Conquest of Arid America* neatly encapsulates arid empire's structure of silence: "It lies there now a clean, blank page, awaiting the makers of history—the goodly heritage of our people."[22] The UA Agricultural Experiment Station was borne of this vision.

AES staffers were initially just as bewildered by the desert environment as the early white farmers in Arizona. But with time, they developed a set of ideas and materials they could share with farmers. They also learned to apply the language and ideals of modern science, becoming fluent in describing the desert Southwest as a *tabula rasa*—a laboratory for exploring the supposedly unknown frontiers of farming in the desert. Their efforts built a self-reinforcing cycle: massive irrigation schemes involved the re-engineering of waterways, which helped settlers with large-scale farming but simultaneously displaced Indigenous communities and eliminated their access to fields and water.²³ In this way, their efforts to justify the AES also ensured the blank-slate idea's longevity: it set Arizona on track for an agricultural present *and* future defined by white settler farmers. Like so many other colonial orators, what all these men failed to mention is that this land was not in fact empty. Rather, their *tabula rasa* story was part of the very process of emptying it of its Indigenous claimants.

In the lead-up to Arizona's recognition as a state, which would not happen till 1912, the territory's political leaders knew that the US's politics of race meant that they needed to establish a firm white majority to win statehood. Simply removing non-white residents would not suffice; they also had to recruit white settlers to colonize Arizona. The University of Arizona's early efforts to promote desert farming highlight an important aspect of how arid empire's power was built and expanded: it relied on advertising agriculture as a modern, lucrative, and promising life path for a new social body.

Early on, territorial administrators tried to recruit more farmer-settlers by suggesting that the desert was an exciting place full of potential riches. From the mid-1800s to the early 1900s, boosterist pamphlets published by institutions like the Chambers of Commerce for Tucson, Phoenix and Maricopa County, Southern Pacific Railroad, City and County Immigration Commissioners, as well as independent "immigration solicitors," all emphasized the opportunities available to farmers from the East who were the desired settlers for state-builders in the Arizona Territory. They aimed to make the settler's move more imaginable by providing hard facts, furnishing prospects with the institutional knowledge to take advantage of the federal government's Homestead and Desert Land laws, which would give them access to farmland in the western territories.

The companies and institutions publishing these recruitment materials were keen to see Arizona populated by settlers from

*Figure 2.4. Mix of Arizona settlement brochures issued by the Arizona Commission of Immigration T.E. Farish (1889), the Phoenix and Maricopa County Board of Trade (1800s), and Southern Pacific Railroad (1906).*

the east because, it was understood, they were white. In his book on Arizona settlement, one self-proclaimed "pioneer," John H. Cady, disparaged the Spanish colonizers' assertion of civilizational superiority that East coast settlers claimed, despite the fact that "the Spaniards possessed fully as white a complexion as the average pioneer from the eastern states."[24] Cady's comments point to a broader debate about racial designations in the Arizona borderlands, where Spanish Americans engaged in a kind of "counteroffensive" against those who described the region as racially "unfit" for statehood by asserting their claims to whiteness.[25] Boundaries around who did or didn't count as white have long been politically charged in the United States, but as Katherine Benton-Cohen bluntly puts it, "Ultimately, agricultural promotion was for whites only."[26]

This dichotomy between white settlers and non-whites was interwoven in the Arizona boosters' definition of a new kind of agrarian idealism in the desert, exemplified in arid empire's unique mastery of the "gospel of irrigation."[27] Of course, Indigenous residents of North America had been practicing irrigation for centuries, and some groups in Arizona like the Pima and the Maricopa were already major commercial agricultural producers by the mid-1800s.[28] Unsurprisingly, the

**Figure 2.5.** *Cover of a brochure outlining US government's Homestead and Desert Land Laws, issued by the Atchison, Topeka and Santa Fe Railway Company (1910).*

colonial boosterist publications tended to be silent on this. In some cases, as in an 1863 publication on "The Geography and Resources of Arizona and Sonora," Indigenous groups were actually framed as a direct obstacle to agricultural development. The author, a military settler in Arizona named Silvester Mowry, describes the Apache theft of livestock and foodstuffs, asserting: "Arizona will have no peace, and her great wealth as a pastoral region must remain undeveloped, until the War Department sends a strong force, and reduces them by fear of absolute submission. They must be fed by the Government, or exterminated."[29]

This overtly genocidal language of extermination had begun to subside toward the end of the 1800s. Instead, the settler recruitment texts started to adopt a more aspirational story, one about civilizing the desert through agriculture. Here, if they did mention Indigenous farming practices at all, they emphasized how white settlers had introduced modern technology that could master desert water capture in a manner that went well beyond what Native communities were capable of. For example, one immigration solicitor pamphlet explained:

> The recent Indians, when discovered by the Spanish conquerors, lived by farming, and then as now their farming was made possible by the artificial storage and carriage of water. Their period may be said to begin with the time when the present ruins along the valley of the Rio Verde were efficient channels watering rich lands, and has been continued to the present day.
>
> What uncivilized Aztecs and barbarian Indians were wise enough to do, white settlers have been shrewd enough to improve upon. Recent as is the agricultural settlement of Arizona, owing to Indian wars now ceased, the Territory can yet present a good list of irrigation systems in successful and valuable operation.[30]

This text reflects a broader settler narrative that framed Indigenous farming and water management as old-fashioned or backward, and the people themselves, as *other*—"barbarian," even.

Meanwhile, the grand scope of irrigation projects undertaken in colonizing Arizona destroyed Indigenous communities' sustainable patterns of water use and farming in the desert, not just by expropriating the water but also by damaging the broader ecological systems they depended on for their livelihoods. This was neither acknowledged nor framed as a problem in the settler stories about irrigation. If anything, controlling the water was explicitly acknowledged to be about establishing absolute control of the land. An 1885 publication on the Salt River Valley makes this explicit: "In desert countries like the valleys of Arizona, *water is king*, and he who owns or controls it becomes dictator, and rules even the cultivator of the soil."[31]

If great wealth reaped from Arizona's soil was a key promise of the recruitment brochures in the 1800s and early 1900s, this quote lays bare the fact that control of the land also required control of the water. Out west, the would-be settler could be more than an entrepreneur—he could be a dictator. The idea of settlers as dictators runs counter to the democratic idealism that glosses dominant American conceptions of Western expansion with the brave spirit of agricultural pioneers and homesteaders. Yet this retrospective nationalist storyline is divorced from the realities of colonization. Indeed, the boosterist materials suggest that dictatorial control might have been useful in selling settlers on a move to the desert Southwest, in part because of the region's association with frontier lawlessness.

Local boosters exerted a great deal of energy—and exaggerated rhetoric—to shake off the "Wild West" stigma and replace it with a different image of agricultural paradise. For example, one publication from the 1800s says of Central Arizona: "It is no longer the frontier—the sweeping wave of civilization has covered it. The cactus has been thrust back and the plain has been made a garden, threaded by great canals wherefrom the farmer draws for the irrigation of his fertile acres."[32] It then goes on to emphasize that the (perceived) threat of Indigenous attacks on white settlers has subsided: "The Arizona Indian of to-day is no longer savage. He is still picturesque, but is rapidly being merged into a most ordinary division of the body politic."[33] Or as a later publication explained:

> The main purpose of this folder is to acquaint prospective settlers with the resources and possibilities of the Salt River Valley. But the resources of Arizona are not confined to this wonderfully fertile valley and a story of the Territory would be incomplete if it did not give an account of the uncounted riches

lying hidden in the hills and the immense values of its lumber. The area of Arizona is so vast and the proportions of its valleys, mountains, and plains so great that the wealth of its resources are but imperfectly appreciated, even by those who have some little knowledge of the Territory. To the stranger, whose ideas of the country have been gathered from newspaper stories, dealing largely with the conditions that prevailed twenty years ago, when Geronimo and his marauding Apaches made life for the occasional settler one round of excitement, the truth comes as a distinct surprise.[34]

Here again we see the effort to substitute the uncolonized image of terror and disorder with the colonized image of Edenic paradise and bounty.

Reflecting the agrarian thrust of US colonization of the West, white immigrants from the East could serve as arid empire's favored agents of nation-building once they were paired with scientific farming techniques and arid lands expertise. As with Jefferson Davis's camel experiment, the US government was so weak in the mid-1800s that colonial leaders looked to any way of projecting power in its new arid empire. White farmers were thus the human building blocks of a new racial geography of the American West, planted on the land to replace its Indigenous inhabitants and the recently ousted Mexican and Spanish occupiers of the land.

Most, if not all, of the Arizona settler recruitment publications were simply silent about whose land their audiences in the East would be settling. Instead, they celebrated the desert as a blank slate, trying to generate excitement among would-be Arizona residents and entice them to imagine all that they could build and grow on this drawing board in the sand. Once emptied and imagined as a space outside of politics, the desert-as-laboratory became a testing ground for the settlers' ideas of modern science, Western ingenuity, and the creative injection of ideas from the Old World to make the New World thrive.

The "Old World" was not Europe, but in fact, the Biblical one: boosterist brochures were filled with references to the Colorado River basin as the American "Nile," which it was said, offered all the fertile land needed for prosperity and progress. To build a new arid empire in the United States, where better to look than the Middle East?

One staple of the Middle East's own agricultural power in its arid regions was date cultivation, which quickly became an object of desire for US agents of empire. The date was an exotic but much coveted fruit in America in the late 1800s. Frank Gulley and the successive directors of Arizona's Agricultural Experiment Station believed that they could build a domestic date industry on the basis of its existing popularity.

While administrative conflicts led Gulley to step down from directing the AES in 1894, his passion for fruit trees remained as part of the AES mission. The next two directors, James W. Toumey and Robert H. Forbes, also became proponents of the university's first experiments with date palms. Gulley, Toumey, and Forbes all worked with private and government agents to import diverse date varieties from around the Middle East through the 1890s and early 1900s. The first decades of AES's work were largely focused on expanding Arizona farmers' capacity for date cultivation.

The date was, in this period, an imported specialty fruit that was much in demand in the United States. Muscat, Oman was, in the 1800s, the center of Arabian date exporting and specialized primarily in the *fardh* variety, which was hardy enough for long ocean journeys. Upon arrival in the US, the dates were not sold fresh but in huge congealed blocks that grocers would then portion off for consumers. Dates were not available year-round, arriving only on ships from the Gulf around Thanksgiving and Christmastime. Americans apparently loved the sweet, sticky treat and it quickly became a beloved part of the American holiday season.

When records of date importing began in 1824 the US imported 44,425 pounds of dates, and these figures increased dramatically over the rest of the century.[35] By 1885, the country was importing more than 10 million pounds of dates annually, growing thereafter to as much as 20 million pounds annually between 1893 and 1903. By 1920, imports were up to 32 million pounds; by 1922, 53 million pounds.[36] Around the turn of the century, grocers were selling millions of pounds of dates during the holidays. With this booming business, the United States had become Oman's most important foreign customer.[37] In 1899, New York newspapers even began an annual "date race" for the first shipping company to arrive from the Gulf with the year's date supply: *would it be the boat from Muscat or Basra?* Eager readers could track the progress of the boats as they sailed, and the winner was feted and awarded a handsome cash prize.[38] The newspapers clearly understood that the hype helped sell papers—itself a testament to the public's passion for dates.

All of this is to say that when Gulley traveled to interview Arizona's white settler farmers in 1890 about what commercial crops they were interested in, dates seemed like a promising and potentially lucrative focus for their arid region. Gulley was acquainted with some of the general characteristics of Arabia's soil and climate conditions, which he believed to have much in common with parts of Arizona. Gulley was also operating within a broader agricultural milieu, which had already begun hypothesizing that the American Southwest would be an ideal place to start commercial date production. The American date industry's early roots in Arizona are all but forgotten, as date production is now almost exclusively associated with Southern California's Coachella Valley in the US popular imagination.[39]

Spanish missionaries had grown date palms from seed at missions in California and Arizona before those lands were acquired by the US in 1848.⁴⁰ After the United States Department of Agriculture (USDA) was founded in 1862, there were some murmurs of interest in investigating the Spanish palm experiments further. But it wasn't until 1882, when the American demand for dates was just beginning to take off, that the USDA finally sent an agent, W. G. Klee, to survey the Southwest and evaluate whether a domestic date industry in the region was viable.⁴¹ Klee's report was positive, but several years passed before he was sent back for a more comprehensive study in 1887. The reports, combined with the skyrocketing date imports to the US, led the USDA to start procuring date palms for testing in Arizona, California, and Texas.

Like Jefferson Davis appointing his men to collect different types of camels from around the Middle East, the USDA tried to get as many different date varieties as possible to test out. From 1890 until 1929, it would import around 20,000 palm offshoots from 149 different date varieties.⁴² The USDA had a "Division of Pomology and Section of Seed and Plant Introduction," which included "agricultural explorers" (a real title) on staff. Part of the United States' long-running project of agricultural state-making, these men traveled the world to collect plant varieties with the potential for kickstarting commercial farming in the United States.⁴³ In a 1900 letter to the University of Arizona AES, for example, the Chief of the Section of Seed and Plant Introduction asked for their requests, explaining:

> Mr. D.G. Fairchild, Agricultural Explorer in the employ of this section, will visit Egypt in the interest of seed and plant introduction during the first three months of 1901. Please inform me whether there is anything which you would like to have him secure for the use of your Station [...]. It would be helpful in planning the introduction of new crops from foreign countries if you would indicate somewhat fully the lines in which we might be of assistance to you.⁴⁴

The puzzle of arid lands agriculture was a favorite topic among USDA staffers, and for decades they focused on importing crops from the Middle East and Northern Africa as the golden ticket to developing commercial farming in the desert Southwest. Date palms received special attention, especially since two of the section's agricultural explorers, Walter Swingle and David Fairchild, were vocal proponents of the crop, even going on to write entire books about dates.[45]

By the time the USDA got involved in palm imports in the 1890s, farmers and scientists knew that date palm seeds could not be trusted to produce palms that bear fruit true to their source. Trees grown from seed can produce radically different plants and fruit from their parent source, and sometimes won't even produce fruit at all. For this reason, the USDA had to import "suckers" or palm offshoots, which grow at the base of a tree. Safely transporting the suckers from the Middle East to the United States was a major challenge because they had to be regularly watered and cared for throughout the months-long journey by boat and rail.

These logistical hurdles notwithstanding, University of Arizona staff worked closely with the USDA's agricultural explorers to secure a special supply of suckers for the university's experiment station. The first shipment of nine palms arrived at the UA Tempe Experiment Station in October 1890, followed in September 1891 by a single palm from the Arabian Peninsula—a Fard, sent by A. Mackirdy, U.S. vice-consul at Muscat.[46] In a letter accompanying the Omani palm, the USDA pomologist made it clear that this was a special favor for the university, and that "no public announcement" should be made because "it would only bring a number of applications when none could be filled."

When the first palm offshoots arrived in Arizona, they looked sickly but were alive. The USDA was anxious about these imports being wasted and regularly wrote AES staff over the next decade to check on the palms' status. Not all

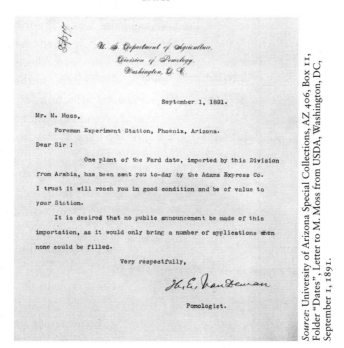

*Figure 2.6. Letter from the USDA Division of Pomology regarding the 1891 Fard palm shipment.*

trees from the first 1890–91 batch would survive, and since AES officials were also anxious about losing their special relationship with the USDA, they were emphatic that any losses were the result of poor packing and shipment methods. James Toumey, who was the AES acting director when the first shipments arrived, was undeterred by the early transport woes and assured the government officials—and the broader scientific community—that the researchers could prevail in their efforts to grow delicious dates in the desert soil.

Like his predecessor, Frank Gulley, Toumey assumed his role as interim director to serve as a staunch proponent of UA date palm research. In 1898, he dedicated an entire AES Bulletin to the date palm, where he explained:

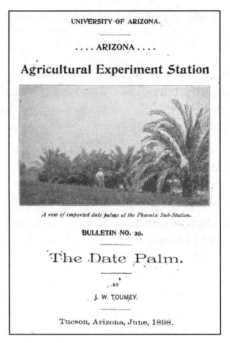

*Figure 2.7.* University of Arizona's Agricultural Experiment Station bulletin dedicated entirely to the date palm.

> It would appear that we are justified in making the statement that Southern Arizona has the requisite climate and soil conditions necessary to grow dates on a commercial scale. This statement is not based entirely upon the similarity of the meteorological and soil conditions of Southern Arizona to those of the date regions of the Old World. It is largely based upon results already obtained in growing the date palm in various localities throughout this region.[47]

That is, for Toumey, their project was not one for dilettantes —it was science grounded in data, measurements, and hard work. And crucially, the lessons of the "Old World" were given new life and significance in the new Arizona desert laboratory. With arid lands agricultural "science" here beginning to take shape, the UA's lab would be the place to show the world that settlers could not just take over the desert but make it productive.

Toumey was optimistic about the AES's scientific contributions to the date industry, but he didn't last long at the helm. He was replaced by Robert H. Forbes, who assumed the AES director-ship in the late 1890s and held the position until 1915. Like his predecessors, Forbes discovered his inner date-palm enthusiast almost immediately. In fact, he took date industry optimism to another level: he would go on to dedicate the next several decades of his career to some aspect of the industry, first in Arizona and later in northern Africa. Forbes was originally from Illinois and trained in chemistry and agriculture. Not long after he moved to Arizona, he married a local woman from a prominent settler family and quickly became enchanted with the desert.[48]

By the time Forbes arrived in Arizona in the 1894, American popular culture was densely populated with romantic Biblical and Orientalist narratives linking the deserts of the US and the Middle East.[49] Forbes was fascinated by these connections and soon became an evangelist for desert-to-desert learning. Like George Perkins Marsh, Jefferson Davis, and the other camel project advocates, he believed the best way to establish control of the new arid lands of the American West was to borrow heavily from Old World desert countries.[50] Forbes looked closely at date farming in the Middle East when he took up the AES's fledgling efforts to start its own date indus-try for the United States. He imagined the Experiment Station becoming a sort of local repository for this knowledge and a conduit for local farmers:

> But in the date growing countries of the Old World the Arabs, and other races, have developed the date until in excellence and variety it corresponds with other cultivated fruits. Knowing that the conditions, especially of climate, enable the tree to

produce in Southern Arizona, it is evidently necessary to avail ourselves of the centuries of Old World experience, bring the best varieties from the Sahara, Egypt and Arabia, and establish them here. This is what the Arizona Experiment Station with the help of the Department of Agriculture is now doing.[51]

Forbes's vision basically involved redeploying agricultural insights of "Old World" communities to the US Southwest, but in a way that would position the AES as innovative, entrepreneurial, and of course, an ally to the settler farmers they were tasked with supporting. "Colonization," Frieda Knobloch reminds us, "is an agricultural act."[52]

One of the most significant contributions that Gulley, Toumey, and Forbes all made to Arizona agriculture was to institutionalize the idea that the desert Southwest was an "American Middle East." The idea predated them, but their work at the Agricultural Experiment Station both reinforced the metaphor and went beyond rhetoric. By actually importing the raw materials—palm offshoots and other crops—and seeing them to literal fruition, they gave life to the trope in the real world. They also illustrated the bigger ideological argument of the colonial policymakers responsible for the Morrill, Hatch, Homestead, and Desert Land acts: that the arid west just needed the right inputs to be brought under cultivation and developed according to Anglo-American visions of civilization.

The AES leaders' romantic portrayals of exotic Arabia also bolstered the idea that American settlers were working with a blank-slate desert on which Old World culture could simply be transposed—all the while continuing to excise the Indigenous peoples and their own agricultural contributions from the land. Instead of recognizing these contributions, Indigenous-settler relations continued to be framed in various university spaces and texts around established storylines of conflict between backwardness and civilization. The cover of a 1900 AES bulletin, for example, reduces the Indigenous perspective to a

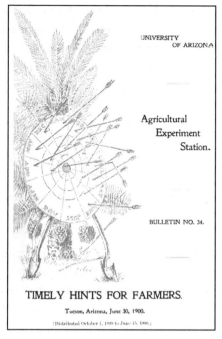

UNIVERSITY
OF ARIZONA

Agricultural
Experiment
Station.

BULLETIN NO. 34.

TIMELY HINTS FOR FARMERS.

Tucson, Arizona, June 30, 1900.

[Distributed October 1, 1899 to June 15, 1900.]

*Figure 2.8.* *University of Arizona's Agricultural Experiment Station
bulletin featuring advice for farms about date palm cultivation.*

singular metonym: an arrow, representing both antagonism
and barbarism, which is lobbed at the new celebrated icon of
settler agriculture in Arizona, the date palm. In many ways,
this oppositional image, juxtaposing "modern" agriculture
with Indigenous resistance, works to increase the spectacle of
the settler storyline of prevailing in the face of great danger
and adversity. The subject of date palms somehow becomes
more titillating when they are under threat.

Early advocates of date cultivation in the Southwest found
allies in the press, who helped to broadcast the spectacle far
and wide. As the trees started to grow, the seductive image
of prolific palms quickly became a prominent theme in the
Arizona boosters' recruitment materials. The media also
reported extensively on the AES work with date palms and

the promise of domesticating this industry. Equally seductive was the image of transforming a desert "wasteland" into a paradise, a trope which the news reports frequently trotted out. In one *Scientific American* article from 1899, for example, the author reports: "It is now proposed by our Commissioner of Agriculture at Washington to make the date a staple American product also. The center of this new enterprise is to be the now useless desert regions of southern California and Arizona. Seed has been procured in Egypt and successfully planted, and more is coming."[53]

Newspaper stories frequently touted the efforts of USDA representatives in traveling great distances to Arabia and Northern Africa to collect the "best varieties" of date palms for import—"on a mission which the department hopes will open a new and profitable industry in the most arid sections of our Southwest."[54] By 1910, the *Arizona Republic* was already congratulating AES Director Forbes for showing that "even the choicest of the old world varieties of dates may be produced to perfection in Arizona."[55] The *Scientific American*'s correspondent concurred some years later, noting that "the faculty at the Arizona university have conclusively demonstrated that dates can be made a profitable crop in the Salt River valley" and that their production figures illustrate that "the arid plains and valleys of the southwest were really fit for something."[56]

When, in 1924, the Date Growers' Institute was established and held its first meeting in Coachella, the date palm was a veritable icon of the settlers' ingenious civilization of the American Southwest through "Old World" agricultural imports. The chairman's opening statement highlighted the impressive speed by which the region went from having just a few "purely experimental plantings" of dates to becoming home to thousands of varieties: "The transposition of date palms from the Old World to the New and the successful establishment on a new and modern basis here in our own Southwest of an industry as old as civilization itself, marks what is perhaps the most wonderful of all great achievements in the realm of Horticulture."[57]

Despite the key role of the AES and other Arizona-based advocates, US date production is now concentrated in California, having surpassed Arizona's production by around 1915. The date industry was set for a steady decline in Arizona after 1950 due to weather challenges, increased production costs, foreign competition, widespread availability of sugar following World War II, and a boom of urban development in the state.[58] But when the AES was actively promoting its date palm experiments in the late 1800s and early 1900s, this work was declared an "unqualified success."[59] The palms proliferated around the state, and photographs of the opulent fruit-bearing trees figured prominently in advertisements for the university and the region more broadly.

While the UA's date palm experiments were being heralded as a "success" in the early 1900s, some obvious losers were ignored in the nationalist declarations of victory: the date producers in Oman and other countries in the Middle East and North Africa. For them, Arizona-based efforts to establish a US date industry marked a process of slow but accelerating

*Source:* R. Rasmessen, 1914.

*Figure 2.9. Postcard of University of Arizona's "Palm Drive."*

decline, and by the late 1920s, the Gulf region's most lucrative export market was undercut by the American crops. A confluence of other factors led the industry to collapse across the region, hitting hardest in Arabia's former leading date market, Oman.[60]

More than 100 years after UA researchers first treated the Arizona desert as a laboratory for Omani dates, the university's involvement in Oman's Million Date Palm initiative stands as a powerful symbol of the trans-regional and trans-historical ironies—and logics—of imperialism. Of course, it is too simplistic to say that the Arizonans "stole" the plant knowledge of the Omanis, only to sell it back to them a century later. Rather, the UA date palm story shows that what the US imperial project did so effectively was to harness the idea of arid lands "expertise" and to package this into its burgeoning higher-education system and the scientific establishment. Through the desert-to-desert connections of the arid empire, first developed in the creation of American scientific "expertise," Omani and other Gulf dates were folded back into this system decades later, which itself generated a new kind of financial, political, and symbolic capital that would become the base of American empire abroad in short order.[61]

Slotting the UA's Agricultural Experiment Station into this bigger colonial story may seem tenuous, especially given that its founding was a stroke of dumb luck when the members of the floundering Board of Regents realized they could be saved by Hatch Act funding. To be sure, these men were lucky. But the confluence of events that allowed the university to found the AES in 1890 was by no means accidental. It was the result of more diffuse structures of power, law, and ideas that underpinned the effort of US policymakers to territorialize the state's authority in the West, where it was still relatively weak and uncertain. The new land and higher-education policies were uneven and unequal, but they nonetheless *worked* insofar as they enlisted the entrepreneurial energies of the statesmen, university administrators, researchers, and farmers to aid in colonizing the Territory of Arizona.

The legal and financial supports given to universities and agricultural experiment stations at this time were also accompanied by the symbolic rewards of recognition. In Arizona, being recognized as a peer in the new community of land-grant colleges running experiment stations was an important step toward being able to credibly don the legitimizing mantle of modern science. The station staff and eventually large portions of the university's researchers were to be recognized as "experts" in arid lands science—beginning with desert farming, but later shifting to include many other aspects of agriculture, water, geology, and climate science. As the early AES directors learned through their work with the date palm, crafting this story of arid lands expertise went hand in hand with crafting the story of the Arizona desert as their dedicated laboratory.

Narrating the Arizona desert as laboratory is only partly about the place itself. Laboratories are also about the people who are imagined to populate them. They are essential sites for individuals to transform themselves into "experts." Working in a particular kind of laboratory allows researchers to claim expert status in a specific domain. In the case of Arizona researchers, a long line of (almost exclusively) men have cultivated this expertise to advance their careers, as well as their personal and political interests. People like Robert Forbes learned to define themselves as arid lands experts to help in the bigger colonial project of establishing state power in Arizona. But just as with Forbes, who went on to serve the Egyptian government, their impact didn't end there.

Many American scientists and technical experts fanned out across the globe, especially to the deserts of the Middle East and North Africa in the first part of the twentieth century. The early directors of the UA Agricultural Experiment Station, who wanted to build a domestic date industry from Arabian imports, may have been the first Arizona researchers to build bridges to the Middle East in the service of sharing knowledge of desert agriculture. But they were far from the last. As we will see in the next chapter, the arid empire that US settlers were building "at home" was soon transported overseas to Saudi Arabia. And of course, as we saw at the beginning of this chapter, UA researchers themselves were back in Oman to build the date palm laboratory, which opened in 2020.

UA eventually closed its first agricultural experiment station in Tempe, with the original date palm site eventually coming under control of Arizona State University. The University of Arizona kept its experiment station in Yuma, however, and it is here that the university has continued to work with date palms and promote date farming locally, largely through the efforts of Glenn C. Wright. Wright came to the University of Arizona from Texas A&M, like Gulley a hundred years before him. And just like Gulley, he too set about learning about local farming interests when he arrived in Arizona in the 1990s. Wright originally specialized in citrus horticulture, but was quickly led to focus on date production in Yuma and became a leading voice in the international community of date researchers and producers. His unique expertise in dates, combined with programs like the Yuma Center of Excellence for Desert Agriculture, has given the University of Arizona a special place among American universities in this field.[62] Indeed, it was precisely this reputation that the Omanis were most keen to tap when they returned to recruit UA to set up a date palm laboratory for their Million Date Palm initiative in the 2010s.

Today's UA presentation of its collaborations in the Arabian Peninsula diverges from the romantic, exoticized constructions of the "Old World" in earlier eras. The institution is now well established and so too is the United States itself, a settler colonial state that does not entertain questions about where its borders begin and end. And yet, lingering questions of who actually profits from knowledge exchanges between Arizona and Arabia persist. In its earliest iterations, America's arid empire was built with Arabian inputs and agricultural knowledge as a resource to be extracted. This is not a story of equal exchange: the Arizona settlers and the imperial agenda writ large benefited most from the agricultural frontier-making that the date palms were brought from Arabia to facilitate.

The date palms were always more than themselves. They were symbols and catalysts: helping pave the way for a different way of thinking about the desert. The "desert," we have seen, can be imagined as a blank-slate laboratory for testing out the ideas and crops of the Old World, or a "wasteland" that can be made to bloom through the wonders of modern science. Yet this is a uniquely depoliticizing image because it directs our attention to the productive crops planted by the white settlers rather than to the processes of colonization and land dispossession that are both past and present in Arizona. The interconnected histories of Arizona and Arabia poignantly show how desert agriculture has been vital to state-making in the American West, and how Middle Eastern materials and imaginaries were key to making this possible.

The story of building empire, of establishing state power, in the western US is inextricably connected with the support of science and institutions of higher learning—specifically tied to agriculture, arid lands research, and desert farming. Political actors, scientists, and farmers all united under a common effort to colonize the Arizona drylands. But the desert wasn't just some passive backdrop that they were working with. Their efforts helped produce the very idea of the "desert" and the desert as laboratory—a special zone of technical intervention that could in turn be operationalized as a site where scientists could travel and develop their scientific credentials. These were credentials that they proceeded to put to work in other parts of the world, then and now.

Arid empire is the silent but ever-present attendant to the date palms that are still ubiquitous at UA and across Arizona's landscapes. Viewing the palms through the perspective of Cressey's "Camel/Coke" double exposure reminds us of the need to question any neat and tidy stories about how they came to inhabit this desert. In contrast to the University of Arizona's story of its early desert farming initiatives as a "noble" scheme to make the desert soils of the American Southwest productive, attending to arid empire shows how institutions of science and their architects are directly implicated in the settler state's project of colonization through agriculture. The leaders at the university were not passive individuals; they were political actors working in the service of the American effort to settle the desert Southwest. And in setting the stage for an "arid lands science," these men found it crucial to master not just the territory but also the idea of the "desert" itself. That is, crafting a convincing narrative about the "desert" and actually claiming desert lands were *both* essential for these agents of arid empire.

# 3

## Diplomacy

*In which we learn about the newfangled idea of desert diplomacy, first tested in titillating agricultural exchanges between Saudi Arabia and Arizona in the 1940s.*

Farmland purchases rarely make national news headlines, but one deal did when the Saudi dairy company Almarai purchased 9,800 acres of farmland near Vicksburg, Arizona, in 2014 for $47.5 million.[1] Almarai, the largest dairy company in the Middle East, planned to use the Arizona farm to grow alfalfa to feed its herd of more than 93,000 milk cows back in Saudi Arabia. Alfalfa's high protein and nutrient value makes it a favored feedstock to rapidly increase cattle size and improve milk outputs, but it is also one of the most water-intensive grains there is. Not all water-intensive crops grow well in the desert, but alfalfa does. It thrives with plentiful sunshine and, as long as the water flows to sustain its growth, farmers can harvest many times in a year.

For the Saudi farm deal in Arizona to make sense, the alfalfa fields needed to have a cheap and reliable source of water. And they did—underground. Thanks to decades-old laws, Arizona's underground water use is controlled through frameworks that designate certain counties as Active Management Areas (AMAs). Where they exist, management plans are based on how local leaders decide the county should prioritize and allocate water. But not all counties are governed as AMAs. La Paz

*Source:* Harrison Koch.

*Figure 3.1. View of Almarai's farm outside of Vicksburg, Arizona. Fields of alfalfa surround the hay collection site at center, December 2019.*

*Source:* Harrison Koch.

*Figure 3.2. One of the new underground water wells at the Vicksburg farm, December 2019.*

County, where Almarai's farm sits, is not part of an AMA. This means that landholders can pump as much freshwater from the underground aquifers as they wish, provided they have a well to do so. When the Saudis took over the farm, La Paz County was quick to issue permits for fifteen new wells, and the company was quick to build them.[2]

Ignoring the financial and regulatory attractions that lured foreign investors to Arizona in the first place, the US media was quick to decry the Saudi "water grab" in Arizona. Almost any Saudi connection is bound to become a nationalistic lightning rod in the United States today, but Almarai's acquisition of the farm seemed especially ominous to critics because the same approach to grain production in Saudi Arabia had already sucked its own aquifers dry ... so much so that the kingdom was forced to ban local grain production by 2018. Now it seemed that the Saudis were coming to do the same thing in Arizona. In the fearful rhetoric of nationalistic American commentators, foreigners acquired farmland to access not just "our" land, but also "our" water.[3]

But if "we" are settlers who took the land and resources from others, such a simplistic storyline is more than hollow—it is deceptive. Since U.S. colonization of the Southwest, settler farmers have appropriated surface and underground aquifer (or fossil) water for commercial agriculture, often in grossly unsustainable and negligent ways. But in the water-grab storyline, such "domestic" uses of the desert's resources are framed as less nakedly extractive than "foreign" uses of the same resources. For example, in reporting on the 2014 Saudi deal, nary a word is said about the fact that, prior to the sale to the Saudis, the Vicksburg farm had already been operating as an alfalfa farm and drawing its water from underground aquifers.

The media fuss that followed Almarai's farm deal points to how naturalized the resource economy of arid empire has become in the U.S.—the "water grab" storyline is its readymade formula to pit domestic actors (i.e., white, non-Indigenous) against foreigners and overlay a moral dichotomy of domestic use/good, foreign use/bad. Nationalist anxieties about "our" water forget the fact that the US itself appropriated the water rights of Indigenous communities in the region not long before. Insofar as they obscure settler colonialism, the "water grabbing" stories extend the broader structure of arid empire. They also overlook a much longer history of US-Saudi ties, which actually gave rise to the very source of the problem: fanciful visions of power and profit from unsustainable desert farming.

In fact, Almarai's purchase of the Vicksburg farm is part of a well-established pattern of agricultural exchanges between Saudi Arabia and Arizona that began in the 1940s. By then, Arizona's burgeoning community of desert farming experts— the ones we met in the last chapter—was ready to move beyond the building of their desert empire at home, and to help build it overseas. If the US could build an arid empire across North America, what would stop it from applying the same lessons to distant desert lands? The scope of arid empire may have once been limited to the American West, but it was quickly transformed into a much grander force as decision-makers in Washington and its foreign embassies started to grasp its potential power beyond North America. Desert stories would now work their magic in the diplomatic world too.

The magnificent dunes that the Arabian Peninsula is known for would not appear to be conducive to much in the way of farming. The region has other landscapes too, but food supply has long been a grave concern among local leaders. As populations grew and lifestyles changed in the first part of the twentieth century, it became even more of a material issue. But it was also a diplomatic issue—one that Gulf rulers eventually learned they could attach to the rivalries of overseas empires. After the collapse of the Ottoman Empire in 1922, the Americans and the British sought a foothold in the Arabian Peninsula, especially as it became apparent that the region had large oil reserves. Imperial agents saw agriculture and natural resource projects as a potential entry-point to the peninsula and a launchpad for their bigger ambitions in the region.

The Arabian Peninsula was not the first overseas target of the increasingly grand visions of American imperialists, but it soon became one of the most important ones. US-based oil companies had already received drilling concessions in Saudi

Arabia by 1933, just one year after the country's independence. Oilmen laid the crucial groundwork for American empire in the Middle East, but they were joined by farmers specializing in desert agriculture. In the 1940s, some of the first American farming experts to travel to Saudi Arabia were from Arizona, where US colonization was not about extracting oil but bringing the arid region under cultivation.

Decades of intensive colonial expansion in the desert Southwest allowed American scientists, farmers, and resource managers to show how they could advance the interests of state-builders in the Arabian Peninsula. As we saw in the previous chapter, these experts perceived Arizona's desert as a strategic kind of laboratory, where they acquired arid lands expertise and fashioned themselves into specialists who could apply their knowhow in any desert around the world. Fore among these skills was how to build elaborate irrigation and pumping networks, and a keen understanding of the political and symbolic power of water in the desert.

American desert expertise was first deployed in an official sense in the Arabian Peninsula with the US-sponsored Agricultural Mission to Saudi Arabia in 1942. The mission was led by Karl S. Twitchell, an American engineer and geologist, who had spent several years mining in Arizona before his first trip to the Arabian Peninsula in the 1920s. In short order, Twitchell befriended King Ibn Saud and became his adviser. Twitchell was an ambitious man, keen for the financial, political, and symbolic rewards that came with serving as a high-level adviser to the king. After the kingdom was established and became an independent country in 1932, he became one of the most influential figures in promoting the partnership between the United States and Saudi Arabia.

Twitchell saw how Ibn Saud was particularly concerned with his country's food supply, and how the king considered agriculture to be an essential part of building the authority of the new state and its royal leadership. The American offered his support for Ibn Saud's wish to modernize farming in his desert lands, and soon set about leveraging his insider status to become the king's liaison with the U.S. government to secure additional support for the effort. Twitchell knew how effective the desert could be in telling a compelling story of commonality between the Middle East and the United States, as ambitious Saudi state-builders mirrored America's own struggle to create its arid empire in the Southwest.

King Ibn Saud's vision for the Arabian Peninsula was just as imperial and far-reaching as that of his new American allies. As Richard Sanger of the US Department of State's Office of Near Eastern and African Affairs wrote in 1947:

> King Abdul Aziz Ibn Saud, the absolute ruler of the predominant heart of the vast Arabian Peninsula, has determined to embark upon a far-reaching modernization of his realm. The early part of his life was devoted to recapturing the lost land of his ancestors. In his middle years he expanded this area until, for the first time in many centuries, the bulk of Arabia from the Red Sea to the Persian Gulf was under the firm control of one man. Now in his maturity, Ibn Saud wishes to develop and consolidate this kingdom he has forged, and to help his people thereby to live fuller lives. He plans to do this by taking the best economic and agricultural techniques that the Western world has to offer, and by applying them to Saudi Arabia in a way that will not upset the basic religious and social pattern of his countrymen.[4]

To realize his grand vision, Ibn Saud turned to his aides, including Karl Twitchell. The two men were conferring in Riyadh in 1940 when, according to Twitchell, the king expressed his interest in mapping the water and agricultural development possibilities in Saudi Arabia's central Najd region, as well as introducing modern "drilling, pumping, and farming equipment."[5]

Ambitious diplomatic entrepreneur that he was, Twitchell proposed that he return to the US to undertake a research mission for the king "over the southwestern states where conditions are somewhat similar to those of Najd."[6] Twitchell's report of his 15,000-mile journey across the American desert was the basis for his subsequent discussions with the king and his advisers about conducting a similar survey in Arabia itself—what ultimately became the 1942 Agricultural Mission. In these early exchanges, Twitchell saw an opportunity to advance both Saudi and American interests, especially through spreading the new American "gospel of irrigation" in Saudi Arabia. Now he just needed the US government to believe his gospel too.

Prodded by Twitchell, the Roosevelt administration eventually agreed to support an agricultural mission in Saudi Arabia in 1942. Over six and a half months, Twitchell led a small team of resource managers with experience in arid lands to assess Saudi Arabia's agricultural potential. US officials, however, were quite clear that they were interested less in the agricultural aspect of the project and more in demonstrating "good will" toward Saudi Arabia, which they hoped would help in securing strategic support—and, ideally, access to airfields—from the king for the US effort in World War II, which the Americans had recently entered.[7] Under Secretary of State Sumner Welles explained it in a 1942 memo to President Roosevelt thus:

> I believe that your message, and the gift of this Mission, will produce a thoroughly favorable effect upon the King, who as you know is the most influential figure in the Arab and Moslem world generally, in and through which a very important part of the war effort is taking place. More specifically, Saudi Arabia lies between the field of activity of the United States Army North African Mission under General Maxwell based on the Red Sea, and that of the United States Army Iranian Mission

under General Wheeler based on the Persian Gulf. The Army Air Corps now has under active consideration the desirability of requesting the permission of the Saudi Arabian Government for the installation of airfields. It is entirely possible that as the result of military developments in the Middle East it will be necessary for our armed services to obtain, sooner or later, rather extensive facilities from the King of Saudi Arabia.[8]

Twitchell was well aware that the US government had grander ambitions than agriculture in mind when it sponsored the agricultural mission, but he was happy for the funding because it allowed him to show Ibn Saud that he could use his influence to get the king certain favors.

Besides gesturing to American "good will," the main task of the 1942 Agricultural Mission's tour of Saudi Arabia was to map and report on its water and land resources for future agricultural development. From May 15 to December 5, the team traveled an estimated 10,700 miles, a figure Twitchell frequently bandied about to heighten the supposed importance of the trip. The mission was joined by various oil company and government representatives at different points, but the core team under Twitchell's lead were men he esteemed for their "many years of varied, extensive experience in the arid and semiarid areas of the southwestern states."[9] These included Albert L. Wathen, acting chief of the engineering branch of the Department of the Interior's Indian Bureau, and James G. Hamilton, a regional agronomist in Albuquerque, New Mexico, for the Soil Conservation Service of the Department of Agriculture.[10]

The mission resulted in a broad-brush report on Saudi agriculture and resources, including recommendations for future developments across the peninsula.[11] Yet it is abundantly clear from Twitchell's personal diaries that the mission was really designed around proposing a major farming project in one place alone: Al Kharj.[12] A spot fifty miles south of the capital,

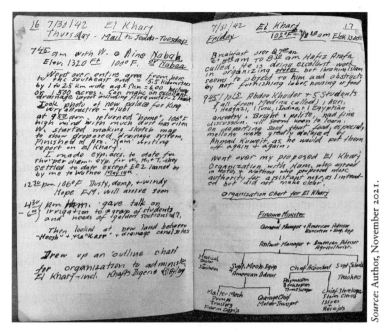

**Figure 3.3.** *A page from Karl Twitchell's diary entries about Al Kharj from the 1942 US Agricultural Mission to Saudi Arabia, Vol. II, in Princeton University's Special Collections.*

Riyadh, Al Kharj was one of King Ibn Saud's favorite escapes and home to a basic but functioning royal farm. Twitchell referred to Al Kharj in his mission notes as the team's "home" or their "home base," reflecting the fact that they would spend a disproportionate amount of time there over the course of the expedition. Twitchell also lavished intellectual energy on the place: whereas his notes from other parts of the country were often spare and included simple lists of natural features, distances, or crops, he wrote extremely detailed and thoughtful diary entries about Al Kharj. By the end of July, he was already drawing up and revising organizational schemes for an American-supported farming initiative there.[13]

It is little surprise, then, that the agricultural mission's survey was followed up with Twitchell championing American support for the royal farm at Al Kharj. This was clearly on his agenda before the 1942 mission commenced, but now he had field observations and scientific data to justify this priority treatment. These were biased observations, of course, but Al Kharj did have some unique natural features working in its favor. Ibn Saud had in fact targeted the region for agricultural production and set up his royal farm there because of its enormous limestone sinkholes, from which aquifer water could easily be tapped. Indeed, these accessible water pits are probably what led my Syracuse geography predecessor George Babcock Cressey to visit in the 1950s. His "Camel/Coke" double exposure image was accompanied by many more photographs of the famous Al Kharj sinkholes, stark testament to the fact that arid lands can in fact hold a wealth of water underground.

King Ibn Saud knew this, of course, and together with his minister Sheikh Abdullah Sulaiman tried to use the water from the sinkholes to develop farming there in 1937. They initially enlisted Egyptian and Iraqi assistance but soon saw that more

*Source:* George Cressey Papers, University Archives, Special Collections Research Center, Syracuse University Libraries (*slide digitally altered for clarity, with permission*).

*Figure 3.4. Overlooking one of the Al Kharj area water pits, slide photograph from SU Professor Cressey's visit in the 1950s.*

Source: T.F. Walters/Saudi Aramco World/SAWDIA.

*Figure 3.5.* Aramco World *photograph captioned, "Arab tractor driver explains problem of cultivating sandy soil at Al Kharj to an American agricultural expert. American farming engineers were brought into Arabia by the Arabian American Oil Company at the request of the Saudi Arab Government. They have successfully taught Arab farmers modern machine farming techniques and methods of crop rotation and use of high test fertilizers."* No date.

technical support was needed to expand operations. The Arabian American Oil Company (Aramco), then a subsidiary of Standard Oil of California, was soon persuaded to take over the farm and import new diesel-powered water pumps and other heavy machinery. By the time Twitchell's Agricultural Mission arrived in Al Kharj in 1942, Aramco had 2,500 acres under cultivation and an additional 1,000 were being prepared for irrigation.[14]

Twitchell's effort to get the Roosevelt administration involved in supporting this farming project represented an important shift in how US diplomatic relations in Saudi Arabia had been conducted to that point: instead of letting the oil company receive the credit for American agricultural benevolence, now it would be the US government. This, Twitchell believed, would endear American politicians rather than just its oilmen to the Saudi leadership. Not long after the 1942 mission, government officials took up Twitchell's idea and sent a team of Arizona farmers, led by David A. Rogers, to take over agricultural operations at Al Kharj in 1944.

David Rogers was the perfect emissary for America's fledgling arid empire in Saudi Arabia. Acclaimed as a desert farming expert by his colleagues in the USDA, he originally hailed from Skull Valley, Arizona. When he was assigned as the Al Kharj project leader, he brought along two hometown friends, Karl Quast and Rahleigh Sanderson, who had also gone into careers in soil science and horticulture.[15] Nearly all accounts of the American involvement in the Al Kharj project mention the fact that Rogers and his farming colleagues were from Arizona, though little else was ever reported about these men. But according to Nils Lind, an American who described his visit to Al Kharj in 1945 for the Department of State, "It is probable that no better group of its size could have been selected, for each member has had years of practical farming experience, largely in Arizona where climate conditions are very much the same as at Al Kharj."[16]

King Ibn Saud was just as rapt with the special skills of these desert farmers and the "Rogers mission" was widely acclaimed as a PR success in the Arabian Desert's Najd region. Lind described a meeting he attended about the project in 1945, when King Ibn Saud told Rogers:

I have confidence in you and now I wish to tell you all that is on my mind—I want you to take over the management of the entire Al Kharj valley. Al Kharj, as a whole, must be known as the American Agricultural Development. There have been too many experiments in Al Kharj in the past, but now you will and must succeed, for anything America undertakes cannot fail. This project is the only important one in all the Nejd, and it must stand as a memorial to American assistance in the Nejd. You will inform your Government of what I have said; and may, also, that I shall send farmers from all over the country that they may see and learn your methods.[17]

Picking up on the same effusive threads coming from the king, diplomat Parker T. Hart, who had opened the US consulate in Dhahran in 1949, remarked: "One must not discount the political impact of the Rogers mission. It was President Roosevelt's penultimate gift to Ibn Saud. His practitioners of desert farming had taken up their mission during the war as a patriotic duty."[18]

The patriotic duty of desert farming was a colonial project in the US Southwest and, as applied to the sands of Saudi Arabia, it was extending America's new imperial reach alongside that of King Ibn Saud. Hart gushed about his Arizona agents of empire:

The mission worked hard in extremely primitive conditions, doing great credit to the US image in Saudi Arabia. It successfully produced excellent wheat and a variety of vegetables without artificial fertilizers. (A 1945 locust infestation wiped out the crops completely, but the team began again and succeeded again.) From the king on down, enthusiasm for the mission spread. Oasis farmers came to inspect the irrigation and to learn how to avoid overirrigation. The quality of the crops impressed them. They also admired the toughness and resilience of the Americans and their hands-on, but scientific, farming methods. [...] The king, who loved the desert and camped in it often with hundreds of his entourage, was a keen farmer and took an admiring interest in the energy, endurance, and wisdom of these Americans of desert upbringing. He not only reassured them that their labors were appreciated, he treated them like his sons. It was a great adventure for the team, and because news in Arabia traveled with astonishing rapidity by human grapevine, word of the success of the American al-Kharj demonstration farm spread far and wide.[19]

The "Americans of desert upbringing" won many friends, and their supporters consistently emphasized Al Kharj as a model for the fledgling Saudi state. The farm was supposed to transfer Arizona knowhow to Saudi Arabia by showing locals how to bring the desert under cultivation. It was thus imagined as a kind of exhibition, showcasing the cutting-edge practices developed in Arizona that could revolutionize Saudi agriculture and introduce "modern" commercial farming to a region in desperate need of food for its population (and the millions of visitors who came yearly for the Hajj). Like the desert-as-laboratory thinking that we saw developed in Arizona in the previous chapter, here the Saudi desert was also treated as an empty space in which modern science and experimentation—and thus "progress"—could be freely deployed.

Ebullient as the Al Kharj project's advocates were, US funding for the project lasted only eighteen months, exposing a rift between officials in Saudi Arabia and their counterparts in Washington. When it came time to renew the funding in 1945, State Department representatives in Saudi Arabia were highly supportive. The US minister in Saudi Arabia, William A. Eddy, sung the project's praises in an airgram to the secretary of state, noting that the king was "emphatic in his praise" of the Rogers mission personnel and that it "attracted favorable attention of everyone."[20] For an extension of any agricultural project to continue past the eighteen-month contract terms, though, Eddy noted: "The agricultural program must be the one the King himself wants, not one devised at a distance and presented to him. The Mission at Al Kharj sets the pattern he wants: An enterprise of the Saudi Government, sponsored and protected by the King, with personnel ultimately responsible to him."[21]

The US government may have been content to support Saudi royal whims at some moments, but the post-war period set in motion a massive financial and geopolitical reconfiguration. In 1945, this was a death blow to the desert farming efforts of Rogers and his men at Al Kharj. The US government could no longer justify this kind of largesse in the desert, especially as American development priorities shifted to reconstruction efforts in Europe. The Rogers team's eighteen-month contract lapsed in 1946, and Rogers himself returned to live in Phoenix.[22] For their part, the Saudis reverted to Aramco for support in keeping their desert farming ambitions alive. Soon, the focus of arid empire in Saudi Arabia would shift from modernization through agriculture to industrial dairy farming.

In most accounts, Al Kharj was described as an "experimental farm." Twitchell hoped that the farm would "eventually become the center of an efficient Department of Agriculture and serve as a working example to teach the most modern practices to landowners and farmers from all parts of the kingdom."[23] And yet Al Kharj was never actually approached as an experiment or model to be scaled up. Rather, the farm was specifically designed to produce crops for the king's personal disposal: most of its produce was distributed to the vast royal family in Riyadh, while grains fed the hundreds of royal horses stabled in the area, as well as other livestock in and around Riyadh.[24]

The fields at Al Kharj produced a wide range of crops, including alfalfa, wheat, barley, oats, and Sudan grass, as well as tomatoes, melons, squash, and more. When Rogers was in charge, he also planted thousands of additional date palms—primarily "improved" varieties developed in California. These traced their own origin to the date circuits from Arabia sixty years prior, but here acquired the sheen of American science and modernity. The State Department's Richard Sanger explained:

> About 10,000 date palms have also been planted in Al Kharj. Although the Arabs have produced dates since time immemorial, new strains and methods developed by the California date growers have been introduced and have increased yields and improved qualities. These methods include careful selection of the stock, the planting of fewer trees per acre, more scientific irrigation, which uses less water than the old Arab methods, and more careful pruning and pollination. Since 1947 the date crop of Al Kharj increased fourfold, and the quality is much improved.[25]

Sanger also emphasized how Rogers's novel approach to farming in Saudi Arabia served as a kind of diplomatic bridge with local communities, helping to overcome cultural and religious divides through something as simple as ... camel dung:

> At first there was resentment in the nearby Arab communities over the intrusion of American unbelievers into the heart of the Moslem world, and the most strenuous efforts on the part of Rogers and his assistants were required to obtain labor. Once recruited, each laborer had to be shown how to perform every elementary operation. These Arabs had never seen a long-handled shovel and tried to cut down those that were given them to the length of their own inefficient tools. Strange as it may seem, the idea of using camel manure for fertilizer had never occurred to them. When Rogers borrowed seventy-five of the King's camels to go about the countryside and collect dried camel dung from native corrals, the drivers shook their heads at the crazy superstitions of Christians. Only the fact that the King had ordered his men to obey the American farmers in every detail prevented a mutiny. Months later, when the ground which had been fertilized out-yielded untouched soil three and four

times, the Arab farmers admitted that there must be something to the practice, and word spread from mouth to mouth about this use of camel dung for something besides fuel.[26]

This civilizational reading of the Rogers team's farming practice was echoed by the American Legation attaché Nils Lind, who wrote up a report on Al Kharj for the State Department in 1945. In it, he recounted his wonder at the precise order that Rogers had imposed on the farm's fields and palm trees, "completely unlike any Arabian project." About 1,500 young palms were spread over one hundred acres with "exactly thirty feet between each palm tree and the rows were straight from any angle." Rogers explained to him:

> In between the palm trees, we will plant vegetables and melons,
> particularly plants which don't want too much sun. Our Arab
> laborers thought we were crazy to plant the palms so far apart,
> but now they [see] our way is better than their helter-skelter
> style of planting. They know palms must have sun and if our
> trees produce better dates than their own, we will have taught
> this country a valuable lesson.[27]

Setting rigid order in contrast to the "helter-skelter" is the hallmark of modernist science, and the Rogers farming approach was built on this vision.

In addition to its impressive modernist order, the spectacle of the farm arose from the dramatic contrast between the lush cultivated areas and the surrounding desert, something that most visitors described as awe-inducing. Local and international press coverage of Al Kharj typically focused on its luxurious watermelons and other impressive fruits and vegetables, which were held as miraculous products of the region's otherwise completely barren landscape.[28] King Saud was quite proud as well, and he would frequently bring visitors out to the farms to show his miraculous produce.

*Source:* T. F. Walters/Saudi Aramco World/SAWDIA.

*Figure 3.6.* Aramco World *photograph captioned, "In 1950. American farm experts and a Saudi Arab farmer discuss the merits of some bumper melons newly harvested from a field near Al Kharj, the farm belt area in eastern Saudi Arabia. Saudi Arab farmers have learned about scientific farming methods and techniques from American agricultural experts brought into Saudi Arabia by the Arabian American Oil Company at the request of the Saudi Government*

Saud once brought with him the leader of Kuwait, whom Sanger reports was apparently so impressed that he soon became concerned that "he would never be able to convince his friends in Kuwait of the size and variety of the fruits and vegetables grown in Al Kharj. When he left, the Americans filled his plane with huge watermelons, cantaloupes, and honeydew melons. The Sheikh sent back word that his friends were so impressed by these samples that they wanted to have a similar project set up in Kuwait."[29] The melons may have been a hit, but the less sensational crops—wheat and alfalfa—were arguably more important for what the Al Kharj region was destined to become: the epicenter of Saudi Arabia's dairy industry and the eventual home of Almarai.

In some ways, the vast fields of forage crops were just as spectacular as a bulging watermelon harvested from the sand, as **Figure 3.6** may suggest. This image, from Cressey's Saudi archive, was included in a 1957 article, "Water in the Desert," which he captioned thus: "This alfalfa field near Al Kharj in central Arabia is a reminder of the way in which irrigation canals may transform an arid waste."[30] Wasteland or not, the desert expertise that the Arizona farmers professed to bring to Saudi Arabia in the 1940s did entail a deep familiarity with farming alfalfa and other water-intensive grains in the desert. In fact, the US government even encouraged two Saudi royal family visits to see these arid lands miracles in Arizona for themselves.

Following from Arizona's earlier history of agricultural boost-erism, cheered on by the UA Agricultural Experiment Station

*Source:* George Cressey Papers, University Archives, Special Collections Research Center, Syracuse University Libraries (slide digitally altered for clarity, with permission).

*Figure 3.7. Alfalfa field in the Al Kharj area, labeled "Water in the desert, Khafs Dugarah, Saudi Arabia," slide photograph from SU professor's visit in the 1950s.*

and its leaders like Gulley, Toumey, and Forbes, the state had developed a reputation for making the desert bloom. In the immigration pamphlets discussed in chapter 2, potential settlers from the East were enticed to move west on the promise of the riches flowing from blooming desert lands, of which alfalfa was said to be "king." The boosterist texts all advertised alfalfa as a kind of get-rich-quick crop—it could deliver huge profits to would-be settlers, and it could make ranching and dairying especially lucrative, thanks to its ability to rapidly fatten the cows.[31]

A standard set of visuals accompanied these advertisements —typically a variation on a prospering field of alfalfa, cows in an alfalfa field, or the harvesting of alfalfa—and the written descriptions also emphasize its importance to farming communities in the West. One brochure from 1907, for example, proclaims:

> If one wants to see alfalfa at home—alfalfa in its glory, falling before the mower six and seven times a year, and green with luscious pasture the first of December and cows feeding on it with great content, let him traverse the Gila Valley, the Yuma, the Salt River or the valleys of the Santa Cruz and San Pedro, as I did. He will see the farmer's side of Arizona, and will see the promise and possibility of a land that only wants good farmers and lots of them.[32]

From the earliest days of American settlement of Arizona, alfalfa had been identified as a key to prosperity in the desert. By the 1940s, it had become firmly established in the state's agricultural economy, especially as its irrigation networks expanded rapidly over the first half of the twentieth century. So when the Rogers team from Arizona traveled to Saudi Arabia in 1944, its members were taking with them a well-established familiarity with the gospel-like promise of alfalfa production in the desert and its special ability to support a livestock industry.

The Saudis were also to encounter alfalfa's celebrity status themselves on two royal family tours of Arizona in the 1940s. In 1943, the royal party consisted of two sons of King Ibn Saud, Prince Faisal and Prince Khalid (each of which would later become king of Saudi Arabia). Their trip included stops in Washington, D.C., New York City, and a short tour around the Southwest. The western leg of their journey received limited media coverage, but where it was mentioned, the stories typically just repeated the official description offered in the State Department press release: that the princes would "visit certain irrigation projects in the southwest portion of the United States."[33] Since the press release was vague overall, no one in the US fully understood the purpose of the princes' trip. Yet newspapers suggested that it was probably because the Roosevelt administration wanted to negotiate further oil drilling concessions in Saudi Arabia and to discuss the situation in Palestine, where King Ibn Saud opposed the growing Zionist cause at the time.

Twitchell, for his part, wanted to have a say in the princes' agenda, and he was immediately on the phone with State Department officials once he learned of the visit. He had only a month to prepare, though, so he threw himself into coordinating several events in New York and outlined an itinerary for the royal tour of the Southwest for the State's Near Eastern Affairs coordinator, Paul Alling. Twitchell, in an unambiguously paternalist fashion, was emphatic that this could not be an unsupervised adventure: that the government officials needed to be careful in showing exactly how the expertise fashioned in America's arid empire out west could be transferred to Saudi Arabia. As he explained in his letter to Alling after their preliminary phone call:

> I believe it is of the utmost importance that full explanations should be made to Amir Faisal and Amir Khalid of what conditions are similar to those in Saudi Arabia, also where the

various places are located in his country which can benefit by
the developments seen at each place he visits. Otherwise he may
wish great projects to be undertaken which would entail huge
expenditures and only end in failure. I feel very sure that a great
deal of benefit may result from his tour if such explanations are
made at and when he visits each locality but great care must
be taken to emphasize what is and what is not, applicable to
his country.[34]

Twitchell did not actually participate in the western segment
of the visit, but it was nowhere near as ambitious as he had
hoped it would be. Prince Faisal and Khalid and their entourage ultimately went to see Navajo sheep-breeding methods in
Gallup and Window Rock, followed by a quick jaunt through
the Petrified Forest and the Grand Canyon.[35]

By now fully committed to his own vision of desert diplomacy, Twitchell was persistent in pushing US officials to
deepen the relationship with the Saudi royal family by inviting them to see the Southwest. But he was not pleased with
this first attempt. He grumbled about its execution afterward
to James Hamilton, of the USDA Soil Conservation Service in
Albuquerque, who had accompanied him on the 1942 Agricultural Mission in Saudi Arabia. Hamilton also felt that the State
Department had botched the visit and lost a huge opportunity
for expanding their desert diplomacy efforts, writing:

I was somewhat disappointed and disgusted in a way with the
itinerary arranged for Prince Faisal and his party when visiting this part of the country. I realize, of course, that everyone
wants to show the other fellow the high spots of his country,
but it seems to me that we could have sandwiched in more
things in an agricultural way that might have some application
in Arabia. [...] We could have spent one day in the Salt River
Valley visiting the Experiment Station, date, grape, and other
fruit plantings [...]. Although I would have much preferred to

have had more time, I think that additional day would have helped a lot and most certainly the party would have been able to have seen something of the agriculture in a country that they were somewhat familiar with and might have possibly carried away ideas that would have ultimately had far reaching results.[36]

While both men simmered in their private exchanges, Twitchell publicly framed it as a great success, and described this kind of exchange as instrumental in advancing American influence overseas in a later edition of his book on Saudi Arabia: "That was the beginning of a very practical American diplomatic policy which may pay huge dividends of international peace and prosperity, not only in our contact with Saudi Arabia but with other countries as well."[37]

Twitchell's vision transformed America's arid empire in Arizona into a showcase for Arabia's own desert empire, built on agriculture and royal control of a contested landscape. In fact, Twitchell had even brought a slide projector and screen on the 1942 mission to show the Saudis images of irrigation and farming projects from his earlier tour around the US Southwest.[38] In short, he valued the art of projecting, literally and figuratively, a story about Arizona's desert, specially curated to the Saudi audiences so they could see the value of cooperation with the Americans. To Twitchell, this was desert diplomacy done well.

A second royal trip to Arizona several years later did a better job of sending this vision home to Saudi Arabia. In 1947, it was Prince Saud al Saud who visited. Given his status as Crown Prince, this trip received much more media attention than that of Princes Faisal and Khalid. But as with the 1943 royal trip, Prince Saud and his entourage were vaguely announced as being on a "tour of agricultural regions of the United States."[39] When the royal party arrived in Phoenix, they were greeted by a full roster of Arizona political notables, as well as by David

A. Rogers, the old Al Kharj farm manager. Rogers, who got to know Prince Saud in Saudi Arabia, was to serve as the local guide to "the agricultural wonders of the Salt River valley"[40] and "the marvels of desert fertility under irrigated cultivation."[41] These marvels included visits to date gardens, fruit farms, alfalfa fields, cattle and poultry farms, dairies, and more.

The Arizona newspapers reported that the crown prince was "interested in agriculture, particularly that of the Salt River valley, where conditions generally parallel those of his own country."[42] He was also shown the Hoover Dam (then known as Boulder Dam) and toured Arizona's water networks. Again, the papers noted his interest in applying Arizona's lessons back home: "He is particularly interested in the irrigation system of the West and the possible establishment of similar systems in the arid land of Saudi Arabia."[43] It was on this trip to Arizona that Prince Saud developed an interest in the cattle and dairy industries, which he later pushed to introduce to Saudi Arabia

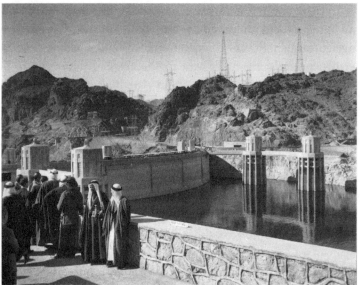

*Source:* Courtesy of Daniel E. Garvey Photographs, Greater Arizona Collection, Arizona State University Library.

**Figure 3.8.** *Crown Prince Saud's party at the Hoover (Boulder) Dam in 1947, captioned: "Party at Boulder Dam from Lake Meade [sic] side."*

via Al Kharj. When the entourage was visiting the Hereford Ranch, the Crown Prince was even treated to a bit of entertainment on demand: "Prince Saud expressed a wish to see a cowboy rope a calf, and one of the Bumstead wranglers went into action."[44]

At the end of all the agricultural touring, Prince Saud was presented with a special box of souvenir seeds. In Phoenix, he had been staying at the Jokake Inn (which has since been consumed by Arizona's ultra-elite Phoenician Resort). Saud was impressed by the desert flowers and plants growing on the Jokake grounds and requested that the seeds be collected to take home to Saudi Arabia. In a small ceremony, Saud was presented with more than a dozen seed varieties, and in thanks he assured his American hosts that they would be planted "in the royal gardens."[45] With Arizona's own seeds headed to the royal Saudi gardens, the local newspapers were overwhelmingly positive about the visit, which they clearly saw as a testament to Arizona's rising status around the world.

Even if the reporting was exaggerated, Saud's tour was an unequivocal success in fostering goodwill with the US agricultural-political establishment—beginning even on the crown prince's first visit with the secretary of agriculture in Beltsville, Maryland. Going well beyond high-level meetings in the DC area, the trip to Arizona allowed Crown Prince Saud to reconnect with his old farmhand, David Rogers. It also fueled his staunch support for the Al Kharj project for years to come. As one visitor to Al Kharj remarked in 1954, "Since his visit to the United States, the present King [Saud] has gone often to Al Kharj and drives around the farms comparing what is being done there with what David Rogers showed him in Arizona."[46] Arizona's arid empire had become a benchmark for Arabia's.

After the US government ended its direct support of Al Kharj in 1946, Crown Prince Saud found ways to keep American support for the project alive. Since Aramco had been in charge

*Figure 3.9.* *Crown Prince Saud's visit to the US in 1947, captioned: "His Royal Highness and Secretary of Agriculture Anderson get hearty laughs out of the performance of a rooster at the Governmental Experimental Farm at Beltsville."*

*Source:* Courtesy of Daniel E. Garvey Photographs, Greater Arizona Collection, Arizona State University Library.

of the farm from 1937 to 1944, Saud went back and persuaded the oil company to take over its management again. Aramco reluctantly obliged and sent some Texas farmers to replace the Rogers team in 1946. When the new staffers arrived, Prince Saud was quick to push them to build a dairy farm like the ones he had seen in Arizona. He wanted a "Grade A Dairy" for Al Kharj, he told Aramco. The new farm manager, Sam Logan from Texas, was put in charge of the project in the 1950s, and he dutifully set to work importing equipment and a range of cattle breeds from the United States.[47]

The Al Kharj dairy was an instant success, and, in short order, Aramco was put to work helping establish two more dairies in the area by 1953. By then, Crown Prince Saud had become King Saud, and he personally owned the Al Kharj dairy. The second dairy farm Aramco helped set up in the area was to be owned by his son Prince Abdullah bin Saud and a third by his longtime adviser, Minister of Finance Sheikh Abdullah Sulaiman.[48] Sulaiman had accompanied King Saud on the 1947 visit to Arizona and was a steadfast ally of the Al Kharj project from its inception. Having an "abiding interest in agriculture," Sulaiman was the main person to enlist American support for the farm years earlier by inviting Karl Twitchell to visit and find ways to expand it—including the agricultural mission and the Rogers expedition that were to follow. According to Twitchell himself, the Saudi agricultural schemes stemmed "entirely from the initiative of the Minister of Finance, Shaikh Abdullah Sulaiman, although naturally King ibn-Saud had to approve the proposals, as nothing of importance can be done without royal sanction."[49]

But Sulaiman found clever ways to exploit the agricultural initiatives for himself. At Al Kharj, this involved appropriating thousands of tons of alfalfa for his dairy, as well as availing himself of the breeding and veterinary services of the farm's staff—something that displeased Aramco auditors a great deal in their reproachful report on the farm's operation and finances in 1954.[50] Whatever Sulaiman's personal interests might have been, he was a vocal proponent of the effort of both Saudi kings (Ibn Saud and Saud) to channel US government and Aramco funds to the Al Kharj project. This, he discovered, was best advanced through a narrative focused on increasing local food production, which would lessen the need for imports and generally improve what would later be termed Saudi "food security."[51]

A few dairy farms would certainly not solve food supply issues in the country, but the narrative served Sulaiman's personal financial interests well. Indeed, Sheikh Sulaiman was iconic of the kind of connected elite who would come to dominate Saudi agriculture for decades into the future—someone skilled at spinning the threat of food insecurity to enrich himself and shoring up his political position in the process. Of course, Sulaiman could not engineer Saudi Arabia's new agricultural landscape on his own; he needed, and had, many allies. What Sulaiman and other Saudi leaders learned at this time was that an international network of technocrats like Twitchell and Rogers was a powerful expedient to build their own arid empire on the Arabian Peninsula.[52]

It was perhaps this network of elite connections that best characterized how arid empire traveled from the US Southwest to the Arabian Peninsula. As one early critic of the Al Kharj project pointed out in 1951, the Americans didn't go to Saudi Arabia to teach the Arabs something new about how to farm:

> Practically everything Americans know about the basic principles of irrigated agriculture was known to the Arabs two thousand years ago. The Americans can, however, apply mechanized power, the use of fertilizers, seed selection, and other new knowledge to an age-old agricultural system and thus point the way to increased yields and somewhat greater self-sufficiency. This, in essence, is the objective of the current Saudi Arabian agricultural program.[53]

Instead, it was precisely the claim to *scientific* arid lands expertise and technology that became essential to the Saudi elite's claim of building a "modern" state. And it was this story of expertise that marked out Arizona's special place in the production of America's arid empire.

The Saudi eagerness to tap into this vision of modernity by partnering with the Americans in the 1940s and '50s dovetailed with the Americans' own interest in advancing its empire overseas. This was not just an arid empire, but an empire built on agricultural modernization. By the 1950s and '60s, this had ossified into a broader movement known as the "Green Revolution," whereby US-dominated "foundations and scientists joined foreign governments and experts to produce new crop varieties that would respond vigorously to a technological package involving chemical fertilizers, pesticides, mechanization, and irrigation."[54] Due to the high cost of the new inputs for "high tech" farming, the innovations ended up helping large farmers and companies, but crushed most small producers. In Saudi Arabia, as elsewhere in the world, one of the major legacies of the Green Revolution was thus to concentrate production into the hands of an ever-smaller number of agricultural elites.

Al Kharj was an early proving ground for the concentration of agricultural power in Saudi Arabia, figuring prominently in these new elite visions of arid empire in the Nejd. The inequalities that the Saudi kings and Sheikh Sulaiman were building into the Al Kharj farms were not often critiqued, but one Dutch diplomat, Daniël van der Meulen, was an exception. In the 1950s, he lambasted the elitist bent of the American model undertaken there, writing:

> In Al Kharj for instance the Americans did not attract the Arab agriculturist but pushed him aside. They wanted large, open spaces for their machinery and any small farmers that happened to be in their way were asked to settle elsewhere. So the American plantations became royal, princely and plutocratic interests. Abdullah al-Sulaiman, the royal family and the few "nouveaux riches" alone profited by it and became the owners of this new type of Arabian "garden." Into the largely democratic Sa'udi Arabia Americans helped to introduce a feudal type of society such as Europe discarded hundreds of years ago. Instead of serving the interests of the governing few, Al Kharj should have been the el dorado of a new type of Arab peasant.[55]

To van der Meulen, the elite-centered approach to agriculture at Al Kharj was the original sin that consolidated Saudi Arabia's future of nondemocratic rule.

Others have subsequently lodged similar accusations, but at this time, no one was pretending to build an egalitarian or democratic system in the Saudi desert.[56] Rather, this was a mission of imperial state making—shoring up the Saudi royal family's authority over space, people, and markets, and ultimately transforming it into a modern authoritarian state. The arid lands technocrats brought from the United States to make the Saudi desert bloom were no democrats either. They, too, were imperialists interested in settling the US West through the gospel of desert agriculture, irrigation, and dairy. Decades later, Al Kharj remains the center of Saudi Arabia's dairy industry. Almarai, the company that purchased the Arizona farm in 2014, is headquartered there today.

A defining feature of arid empire is how its power structures work through a politics of invisibility. This is what Cressey's "Camel/Coke" juxtaposition reminds us to bear in mind—that all that is visible in one moment belies a wider set of invisible networks of power and possibility. The agricultural networks set in motion at Al Kharj continue to be difficult to see in Saudi Arabia, but they remain just as transnational as when they started with the arrival of foreign farmers to tap the region's famous sinkhole water reservoirs and cultivate the desert. The broader logic of harnessing *foreign* resources—machinery, materials, and people alike—to promote *domestic* food aims was something that the first Saudi kings and their advisers learned early on. From the beginning of the Al Kharj project to Twitchell's Agricultural Mission and beyond, Saudi leaders deftly mobilized these international connections to access food-related aid from their new allies in the United States, before, during, and after World War II.[57]

Agro-commodity circuits today are highly globalized, encompassing not just basic agricultural inputs like seeds and fertilizer, but also include a transnational network of storage, processing, trade, and logistics.[58] The invisibility of these supply chains is what makes it so hard to apprehend how a Saudi dairy company like Almarai draws on a wide range of foreign imports, like alfalfa from Arizona, to keep it running. But Almarai is emblematic of how far-reaching Saudi agro-commodity companies have become. Now the largest dairy company in the Middle East, Almarai has expanded into many other categories including juice, baked goods, and infant formula. It also manages a massive logistics network of vehicles, port facilities, and shipping for the distribution of food, grain, and more.[59]

Almarai was founded in 1977 by Prince Sultan bin Mohammed bin Saud Al-Kabeer (who remains with the company as the chairman of its board) with the support of two Irish brothers, Alastair and Paddy McGuckian. The company's farms were initially scattered around Saudi Arabia but were later consolidated around several "super-farms" in Al Kharj.[60] Al Kharj's strategic location above Saudi Arabia's major aquifers have made it a favored destination for the water-intensive activities of grain production, livestock management, and dairy production for many years. Yet the region was not automatically destined to become the seat of a massive dairy industry. Rather, this came about because of how its resources and history combined with Saudi food policies and subsidies that stemmed from those early American interventions in the 1940s and '50s. There was another important American contribution to the story, too—the elevation of anxieties about the security of Saudi Arabia's food supply in the 1970s.

From 1972 through '75, a major world food crisis led to a doubling or tripling of prices for internationally traded grain, accompanied by famine across much of Asia and Africa, as market and political forces united to run down grain reserves and drive up prices.[61] At about the same time, OPEC countries, including Saudi Arabia, imposed an oil embargo that crippled US oil supplies. That 1973 oil embargo led President Richard Nixon to threaten to use a "food weapon" against OPEC members by imposing a grain embargo in response.[62] Nixon's threat was basically unenforceable due to the vast array of global sellers who could subvert such a US embargo, but the very idea caused great consternation in the Arabian Peninsula. If nothing else, regional leaders felt pressured to develop policies that at least *looked* like they were undertaking a serious effort to protect their countries' food security.[63]

In Saudi Arabia, the food crisis and embargo threats combined to precipitate a massive subsidy program directed toward grain production, along with vast funding to import cattle and buy milking machinery. Following on the legacies of the Green Revolution and Saudi Arabia's general state-building project of concentrating political and economic power in the hands of relatively few, the subsidy programs benefited big farming conglomerates and continued the decades-long trend of quashing small-scale farming across the country.[64] The ecological implications of this scheme were just as predictable as the social ones: the rapid depletion of underground aquifers as water was pumped to vast grain fields.[65]

Just like the American desert farming schemes in the Southwest, ecological concerns weren't considered in this thrust of Saudi Arabia's own arid empire. The short-term perspective was what mattered: the Saudi government was winning key allies among farming elites, who were in turn reaping the generous rewards of the state's extraordinary subsidies. As some observers put it in the early 1980s, "It is not surprising that there is a bonanza air present in many parts of Saudi Arabia."[66] Indeed, the bonanza led Saudi Arabia to became one of the world's largest wheat exporters. Its wheat production skyrocketed from 3,300 tons in 1978 to over 3.9 million tons in 1991.[67] The generous agricultural supports could only last as long as the water did, and the environmental reality they were built upon was inherently unsustainable. The consequences were nothing short of disastrous, as the country's aquifers were decimated—something critics had warned against long before 2008, when the Saudi government officially recognized that a crisis point had been reached.[68]

*     *     *

The year 2008 saw a marked rhetorical and political shift about water and agriculture policies in the kingdom. Partly, this was tied to the mounting evidence that the country's underground water was simply running out. It was also related to yet another global food crisis, which started in 2006. Like the 1970s, a rapid and dramatic inflation of food prices buffeted the world. That put economic pressure on the Saudi government budget, and that, in turn, led the country's leaders to worry about potential popular upheaval. Together, these circumstances finally triggered the Saudi government to transform its domestic food production. Saudi agricultural aspirations were always built on limited water supplies. The fundamental challenge of its arid empire, modeled so assiduously by the American experts who sought to entrench white settler control of the Southwest through desert farming, was precisely the immovability of the political relations it represented.

All along, a major sticking point in reshaping Saudi agriculture was the fact that the decades of subsidy schemes had created a powerful agricultural lobby intimately tied to the country's largest capital groups. Government insiders soon understood that any change in agriculture policy carried a high risk of alienating important regime allies. So when it became clear that the country was running out of water and could no longer subsidize domestic grain production, government insiders felt that they could not simply cut off the flow of cash to the agricultural elites. Instead, they shifted the agricultural subsidy programs to support foreign farmland acquisition and otherwise sourcing grain abroad.[69] Almarai was one of the major agricultural players that benefited from this new policy, both starting to acquire foreign farmland and shifting its business models to become a more diversified agro-commodity conglomerate.[70]

Meanwhile, 2008 also marked the Saudi government's first incremental steps toward phasing out domestic grain production. By the end of 2018, a complete ban on growing green forage was in place. These new policies essentially undid the work of Rogers and his successors at Al Kharj decades before. And yet not all was undone. The government didn't go so far as to dismantle its enormous dairy industry: the cows could remain. Their feed had to be sourced elsewhere, however, which is what led Almarai back to Arizona in 2014. From their own experience, the Saudis knew that a desert setting is ideal for a crop like alfalfa, which grows extremely fast when the sun is plentiful. As long as their farms had cheap and accessible water, a desert farm would mean the biggest bang for their buck.

When Almarai was searching for farmland in 2014, Arizona's rural hinterlands fit squarely in the profile of attractive places to source alfalfa. The state's long history of political support for farming helped, but so did the fact that Arizona's groundwater pumping is unregulated in La Paz County, where the Almarai farm is located. The dizzying patchwork of water laws has meant that even critics of new farmland deals in Arizona have felt powerless to mount any meaningful opposition. The sense of political paralysis prevailing in the region is convenient for the Saudi investors. So too is the state's bountiful sunshine, which means more alfalfa can be produced per acre than anywhere else. This is, of course, what the boosters of territorial colonization in Arizona had been saying since the 1800s: "Alfalfa is king!"

The earliest advocates of alfalfa production in the US Southwest were quick to cite the tonnage produced per acre and proclaim the miracle of irrigation, but the finitude of water was carefully omitted. This would indeed be an inconvenient headline (or even footnote) for the celebratory rhetoric used to invite white settlers to Arizona, but the state's colonization was ultimately founded on the myth of abundance. And it was this same myth that David Rogers and his team of Arizona farmers were selling when they went to harness the Saudis' own underground water to irrigate new wheat and alfalfa fields at

Al Kharj. The fact that Almarai is the company returning to now pump Arizona's aquifers for its own alfalfa is another of the trans-regional and trans-historical ironies of arid empire, like the Arizonans returning to Oman to sell their date palm expertise.

Arid empire's double-imperial project does not accommodate easy victim/victimizer storylines, as with the sensational "water grab" reporting on Almarai's purchase of the Vicksburg farm in 2014. Perhaps one day the new Saudi wells at the farm will go dry; for now, though, Almarai's Arizona farm is a quiet place. When I visited in 2019, the impressive new wells were whirring away, pumping fossil water up from deep below my feet. The resident cows calmly rested in the shade and an occasional truck heavy with hay rumbled by. Locals occasionally heckle their leaders at community meetings, but most go on about their business without attending to the Saudi funding that supports their area—or the role their predecessors played in helping lay the groundwork for the mega-dairies of Al Kharj, whose cows their alfalfa now feeds.

The history that underpins the ordered serenity of Almarai's Arizona farm is little known. This is because arid empire harnesses the modernist inclination for order and simplicity to obscure its multi-directional flows across time and space. Singular stories, of past and present, of us and them, of victims and villains, play on the comfort that simplicity offers. Singular vision is easier on the eye, the mind, the conscience. It is easier, at least, than the double vision that is needed to perceive arid empire's evolution over time and space. Yet arid empire's virtual invisibility did not slow its expansion. As the circuits of desert diplomacy expanded in the 1940s, flows of men, expertise, and imperial ambition grew—and with it, America's influence in the Arabian Peninsula.

# 4

## Desal

*In which we track arid empire through the
turbulent terrain of post–World War II
decolonization and the Cold War, when
America's arid imperialists pushed the fanciful
(and arrogant) idea that Arizona's expertise could
"cultivate" modernity in the Arabian Peninsula.*

There is something astonishing about seeing an oasis of
greenery in a desert or to see produce growing in a seemingly
infertile land. But the seductive allure of the oasis is built on
its inverse: the terrifying image of a water source running dry.
The image of dry seas, dusty riverbeds, and depleted aquifers
frightens anyone who lives in an arid climate. For some people,
however, this fearful image is interpreted more as a challenge to
human ingenuity—one that merely needs the right technology
to overcome environmental limitations. Such techno-optimists,
as they can be called, have dreamed up many ways to provide
abundant water to make the desert bloom, such as mechani-
cally pumping underground aquifers or desalinating seawater.
As the previous chapters have shown, arid empire depends on
much more than the strategic control of natural resources; it
also requires the networks of power and expertise that put
the desert's resources to work in service of empire. During the
global wave of decolonization after World War II, however,
the shape of empire—both its ambitions and anxieties—
underwent a dramatic transformation.

After the end of World War II, formal empires were dismantled in fits and starts. Decolonization picked up across Asia, Africa, and the Middle East over the span of several decades and, along with it, the American concern about how newly independent countries would align themselves in the Cold War order. Cold War geopolitics was rooted in a binary worldview that pitted a democratic, capitalist camp led by the US against a state-controlled, communist camp led by the Soviet Union. This was first exemplified in Winston Churchill's famous 1946 "iron curtain" speech, when he warned that a "shadow has fallen upon the scenes so lately lighted by the Allied victory," as Soviet influence grew in Eastern Europe. Churchill asserted that the United States now stood "at the pinnacle of world power" and that the post-war reordering was "a solemn moment for the American democracy. With primacy in power is also joined an awe-inspiring accountability to the future."[1]

Many Americans became enamored with Churchill's dramatic message of great power, which fit neatly with the country's long history of imperial zeal in colonizing North America and then building its own formal empire overseas.[2] But how was the US to approach this imperial responsibility for the future when traditional empires were supposed to be relegated to the past? How could the country keep up the image of a democracy that it used to attract decolonizing countries to its side and away from the communist Soviet bloc? The evolution of arid empire during the Cold War provides a window into some of the ways that American influence expanded and evolved in the time of decolonization.

Building on their early success in mobilizing Arizona's arid empire, UA researchers were quick to adapt to Cold War opportunities and advance their work through the channels of scientific exchange rather than those of formal empire. Though their arid lands focus was unique, they were part of a broader structure of informal empire that developed as American influence spread overseas in the post–World War II era—one that happily enlisted valiant scientists in the Cold War fight against communism.

Higher education was a major beneficiary of the new Cold War infrastructure in the United States, which included huge new pools of government funding for research, as well as the expansion of philanthropic foundations and nongovernmental organizations aimed at expanding US influence abroad through science, development aid, and other modernization schemes.[3] The new funding opportunities sparked an increasingly entre- preneurial environment in American higher education, and academics and their institutions were increasingly pulled into the orbit of American nationalism that gathered strength during the Cold War. Many scholars willingly positioned them- selves and their careers in service of the ensuing Cold War agenda, heeding political scientist Harold Lasswell's famous call in 1951 for social scientists to use their scholarly networks to advance US interests abroad.[4]

The research community was thus mobilized to spread the country's imperial vision not through the language of empire but through the language of science. As elsewhere across the US, University of Arizona leaders were eager to avail them- selves of the new revenue sources that grew out of the Cold War: there were rewards to be had in re-narrating the desert story as a weapon in the American fight against communism. By the 1950s, the university had become a hub for the bur- geoning field of "arid lands studies," which began to take shape after UNESCO's introduction of an International Advisory Committee on Arid Zone Research in 1950. The UNESCO framework served to unite a growing international commu- nity of scientists working on arid lands, while new funding sources helped institutionalize domestic research on deserts in the US. For example, the University of Arizona formed its own Arid Lands Committee after receiving a $208,000 grant from the Rockefeller Foundation in 1957. The committee was then formalized as the Office of Arid Lands Studies upon receiving a $250,000 grant from the US Army in 1964.[5]

By 1969, UA President Richard Harvill was welcoming attendees of the International Arid Lands Conference to the university's campus in Tucson, boasting:

> We are proud of our record of achievement in studies of nearby and far-away arid lands, but we are prouder still of the many students we have prepared here—men and women whose special skills have contributed much to the solution of problems of our own and other arid regions. The hundreds of students we have prepared here—those from the Rajasthan, the Negev, the Karroo, the Chihuahuan, the Namib and elsewhere—have, we hope, returned home to create, through science and technology (and the humanities as well) a society in keeping with modern man's belief in his individual worth and his place in the sun. […] It is good to know that on every continent, other men, many of whom are here today, are devoting themselves to the increase of knowledge—knowledge which will deepen our understanding of the interacting elements of the desert landscape: its exploitable wealth, its productive potential, its human needs, its transcendent beauty.[6]

In short, for Harvill, expanding the frontiers of science and international cooperation was key to unlocking the riches of the desert. From the perspective of UA leadership, the university's desert location was also key to unlocking the financial and reputational rewards of cornering the market on arid lands expertise. Fortunately for the administrators, they had already been collecting a diverse range of techno-optimists, who passionately believed they could engineer their way out of any environmental limits to life in the desert—water scarcity included.

The earliest technological advance in the cultivation of Arizona and Arabia's arid landscapes were wells that could

*Source:* UA Special Collections.

**Figure 4.1.** *"Irrigation pumping plant, Yuma, 1897. Pumped 21,000 gallons per minute making it largest in United States then. Jasper Parvin is the engineer."*

be pumped electronically, replacing the slow and expensive animal-powered methods of the past. In Oman, Saudi Arabia, and Arizona alike, clever canal systems could divert water to crops far from the original source. Extracting freshwater from wells and canals was still limiting, though. The real promise of limitless water is in the ocean. Optimistic engineers, farmers, and seafarers have long sought ways to make saltwater usable through desalination—that is, stripping out the salt.

Water desalination is an ancient practice, based on various techniques of distillation. European explorers began trying to modernize it in the late sixteenth and early seventeenth centuries, when they installed emergency desalting devices for their long ocean voyages.[7] The practice was later expanded aboard steamships in the 1840s and '50s and quickly transformed into land-based desalting facilities built around steam condensers.

Modern desalination (or "desal") plants have evolved vastly since then, especially with the introduction of reverse osmosis ("RO") technology that shoots the water through semipermeable barriers to remove the salt. Whether desal plants use distillation or RO, they still require tremendous energy inputs, either to heat the water for the condensation process or to funnel it through the RO membranes. This has led to a vast array of engineering proposals for how to power water desalination, ranging from the earliest uses of fossil-fuel-powered steam condensers to later proposals for the use of nuclear and solar power.[8]

In Arizona, a group of techno-optimists began working on this issue in the 1950s under the University of Arizona's Environmental Research Laboratory (ERL). The ERL began as the Solar Energy Research Laboratory, setting up a paired greenhouse-desalination project in Mexico. The idea was to use water desalinated through solar power to grow food for coastal desert environments. The UA laboratory got its new name —swapping out "Solar Energy" for "Environmental"—after it became clear the lab wouldn't be able to desalinate seawater using solar power. Despite this early setback, the ERL's leaders were ambitious, and they found a receptive audience in the Arabian Peninsula.

Cities in the Arabian Peninsula could begin to grow only with the introduction of large-scale desalination facilities. Today, they rely almost exclusively on desal for their water needs. Due to the high cost of desalinating seawater, however, the region never used treated water for commercial agriculture: it was always more efficient to import food. Or in the case of select spots like Al Kharj and parts of Oman, local agriculture could be developed by tapping underground water reserves. Yet the Arizona project in Mexico promised a new model, which might make it possible to develop the agriculture sector in coastal regions of the Arabian Peninsula—or so the ERL leaders promised Sheikh Zayed of Abu Dhabi in 1968. Abu

Dhabi was then an emirate of the British Trucial States, and later became the largest emirate in the United Arab Emirates (UAE) after gaining independence in 1971.

The ERL's desal-farming project in Abu Dhabi has largely been forgotten today, as it was dismantled less than ten years after it began. But when the Arizona researchers began marketing a vision of transforming Abu Dhabi from a desert "wasteland" into a productive agricultural hub in the 1960s, they were continuing the American practice of arid empire—packaging and selling their desert expertise in the name of a grand, techno-optimistic future, while reaping a nice profit. They worked alongside local leaders in their state-making efforts on the cusp of independence and helped advance the American vision of arid empire in the Arabian Peninsula. As the ERL's trials and travails in Abu Dhabi suggest, though, this was not a smooth or unidirectional process. Arizona's arid lands experts at first succeeded in selling their story about modernizing the desert in the UAE, but they quickly learned that the story was not theirs alone: it was one that the Emiratis could and would use too.

Prior to becoming an independent country in 1971, the UAE consisted of various small emirates known collectively as the Trucial States—so-called for their truce- or treaty-defined protection from the British Empire that began in 1820. The British government claimed exclusive territorial and commercial control of this part of the Arabian Peninsula's coast, but as elsewhere in their empire, they were less concerned with local development than with achieving their own political, economic, and security objectives. After oil was discovered in the 1930s, British agents felt that they needed to do more to legitimate their new interest in extracting the region's resources and began supporting limited projects that would address local concerns. For Gulf Arab leaders, water and food supplies were at the top of the agenda.

The Trucial States' desert hinterland beyond the Gulf coast is dominated by vast sand dunes and a few sparsely populated oasis towns. Receiving four inches of rain per year or less, this extremely arid desert forms part of the *Rub' al Khali*, or Empty Quarter, made famous in the West by early-twentieth-century colonial explorers and traveler-writers such as Bertram Thomas, St. John Philby, and Wilfred Thesiger.[9] British writers set the Arabian Desert's reputation for being harsh and forbidding to all life, so perhaps it was unsurprising that the imperial agents did little to support agriculture in the Trucial States, even though they were at great pains to do so in other parts of their empire.[10] Perhaps they didn't quite know how. It is certain, though, that they didn't have a proper map of the region's physical geography.

In the middle of the twentieth century, colonial officials started to suggest that the region's lack of agricultural development was the result not just of climatic, labor, and technological limitations, but also because land and resources had not been surveyed. Only with a map could they have actionable information. British officials thus began commissioning land and water surveys, and in 1955, they began their first model agricultural settlement in the emirate of Ras Al-Khaimah. Known as the Agricultural Trials Station in Digdagga, it was said to showcase modern farming techniques and to help local farmers envision a commercial future for the region. Yet British authorities saw the project as a way to "win hearts and minds" in the Trucial States following the Saudi occupation of the Buraimi oasis and nearby territories from 1952–4, during which the Saudis criticized the British for failing to promote local development.[11] Although the British eventually intervened to resolve the conflict, they started to worry about their image among locals. The farm was thus imagined as an illustration of British benevolence —but without being so expensive as to upset increasingly cost-conscious Treasury officials in London.

Digdagga staff were initially charged with educating local farmers about Western cultivation methods and testing out different fruits and vegetables for potential commercial production in local markets. Later, in the 1960s, they worked to develop bovine dairy farming for the first time in the UAE. Yet the Digdagga Station's impact was extremely limited. The British agent in charge of it was reluctant to do outreach with local farmers and the produce itself did not circulate widely because of limited production, means of transport, and colonial authorities' disagreements about whether goods should be marketed and sold at all. Colonial administrators far away in Bahrain and London were constantly squabbling about Digdagga's utility and financing. In one Foreign Office memo, an exasperated officer reacted to a discussion about its future, explaining that "Her Majesty's Government cannot be expected indefinitely to go on subsidising a model farm on which nobody models himself."[12]

Digdagga was not, in short, the PR victory that the British had hoped for. Nor did it do much to advance agricultural production in the Trucial States. It was thus that by the 1960s, commercially oriented agriculture had not reached any of the other emirates beyond Ras Al-Khaimah. Fresh produce remained available only by import, and assessments of Emirati agriculture in the 1960s and '70s were uniformly bleak.[13] This state of affairs is what the University of Arizona's Environmental Research Laboratory supervisor—a techno-optimist par excellence, Carl N. Hodges—found when he was selling his vision for a unified desalination-greenhouse project to Sheikh Zayed, Abu Dhabi's new leader since 1966. Like the Arizona men who had traveled to the Arabian Peninsula before him, Hodges's ambitious dream to transform the desert into a productive agricultural hub was tied to his arid lands expertise first honed in America's own arid empire. Unlike those before him, however, his high-tech offering was to be desalination.

Born in 1937, Carl Hodges began graduate studies at the University of Arizona after receiving a UA undergraduate degree in mathematics in 1959. In 1961, he was hired as a research assistant for the university's new Solar Energy Research Laboratory, which was established in 1955 by A. Richard "Dick" Kassander. Kassander was an entrepreneurial man—a trained physicist and a budding UA administrator. And he took a particular liking to Carl Hodges. Not long after hiring the young man, Kassander appointed Hodges as laboratory supervisor in 1963, despite the fact that Hodges was only twenty-four and had not even completed his graduate degree. In fact, he never would.[14]

It is unclear why Kassander placed so much confidence in Hodges, but it *is* clear that the elder man saw Hodges as a kind of protégé. An intimate and paternal relationship between them blossomed. A series of PR photographs for the Solar Lab's first major desal project in Mexico—one of which is in **Figure 4.2**—put this relationship on full display. The elder Kassander looks on, almost lovingly, as a youthfully handsome Hodges kneels and submissively attends to the equipment, turning a knob or holding a cup to the water spout. In a short *Spectrum* PBS documentary featuring the lab's work in Mexico, "Sun, Sand, and Sea," the two men's affection is palpable: Kassander looks on approvingly as Hodges starts to explain the desalination technology they were working on.[15] Hodges didn't stay a beautiful golden boy for long, but this was the beginning of a close bond that lasted until Kassander's death in 2017.[16]

The UA Solar Lab received a grant to begin work with the University of Sonora in Puerto Peñasco to build a solar-powered desalting plant in the early 1960s. Funding first came from the US Department of the Interior's Office of Saline Water (OSW), but Kassander soon drew on his connections at the Rockefeller Foundation to secure additional support to pair the desalting plant with plastic-covered greenhouses.[17] Their basic idea was that these paired desal-greenhouse facilities

*Source:* University of Arizona Special Collections, UA Bio, Hodges, Carl N. 1937–

*Figure 4.2. Richard Kassander (left) and Carl N. Hodges (right) at the UA Solar Energy Research Laboratory in Puerto Peñasco, Mexico, 1964.*

could be built in coastal desert zones all around the world, simultaneously solving both food and water challenges in arid regions.

The only problem was how to power the system. Entrepreneur that he was, Kassander was keenly aware of the importance of selling the story of a solar solution for coastal deserts' water desalination and agricultural needs. Without solar power, desalination for the greenhouse component of the project would not have been economical. As noted already, the energy demands for desalinated seawater is a major reason that the Arabian Peninsula's coastal regions had never developed commercially oriented agriculture. Hodges and Kassander hoped to engineer a solar solution, but they never did succeed on this account, and the facility was instead powered by diesel engines. This didn't stop them, though, from misrepresenting their work as a success: in their advertisements for UA's desal-greenhouse project, both men often (though not always) erroneously depicted it as solar-powered.

Hodges quickly fell in love with the limelight and reveled in being characterized as a "boy wonder" or "wunderkind." Kassander too was eager to promote this characterization of Hodges for reasons that are not entirely clear. Nonetheless, there are many cases in the University of Arizona archives showing Kassander advocating for Hodges, often unduly or in an effort to secure him undeserved status. At one point in 1968, for example, Kassander pushed UA president Richard Harvill to allow Hodges to receive a doctoral degree in "Water Resource Administration" over the opposition of the university's Graduate Council and Advisory Council, and after having failed his Master's-level exams.[18] Ultimately, Kassander's efforts proved futile, to Hodges' lifelong chagrin. So while he never received his graduate degree, the primary ticket to being taken seriously in academia, he became adept at harnessing his youth and handsomeness to sell himself as a "visionary," and reaped the personal, financial, and political rewards like the perfect grifter he was to become.

Together, Kassander and Hodges ensured that the UA Solar Lab's Mexico project received ample press coverage in both popular media outlets and science journals. It was profiled in a 1967 issue of *Time* magazine, which heralded Hodges as a man of action and foresight:

> Although the oceans lap at their shores, more than 18,000 miles of the world's coastlines are virtually uninhabited because of the lack of available fresh water. Visionaries have long dreamed of using sea water to make these deserts bloom, but University of Arizona Scientist Carl Hodges is actually doing something about it. And not by means of futuristic and costly nuclear-powered desalination plants, but by efficient use of simple diesel-electric engines like those that now provide power to remote communities all over the world. A pilot project on

Mexico's Gulf of California is already accomplishing in miniature what Hodges hopes to achieve on a global scale.[19]

The article may have exaggerated Hodges's innovation, but it
is honest about the fact that the Puerto Peñasco project never
ran its desalting process on solar power, instead using diesel
engines. This detail might have been a deal-breaker for some
decision-makers considering adopting such a scheme, but not
for the oil-rich leader of Abu Dhabi, Sheikh Zayed.

The *Time* article was a turning point for the ERL because it
was how Zayed learned of the UA's project. An aide of Sheikh
Zayed allegedly got hold of this article and, according to one
newspaper reporter, shared it with Zayed, who "became so
excited at the possibility of having fresh vegetables grown in
his country, which has an annual rainfall of 1 inch, that he
invited the director of the research station, Carl N. Hodges,
to Abu Dhabi."[20] Hodges and his team from the ERL visited
shortly thereafter, and were quick to agree to the emir's request
for one of his own.

Building on the decades of experience covered in the previous chapters, these Arizona farming experts found a welcome
audience in Abu Dhabi, where local leaders shared similar anxieties as their Saudi neighbors with respect to food and water
supplies limited by the region's desert environment. By this
point in the 1960s, UA researchers and affiliates had become
savvy in the art of selling their arid lands expertise. They could
easily point to their Arizona context to emphasize how this
endowed them with a unique knowledge of desert farming,
water, and other arid lands infrastructural challenges. To win
high-dollar contracts (and prestige), Hodges, Kassander, and
the ERL emphasized their ability to solve these challenges
because, after all, they were drawing from nearly a century of
technical expertise in cultivating the US's arid empire in the
Southwest. After all, how different could the Arabian Peninsula be?

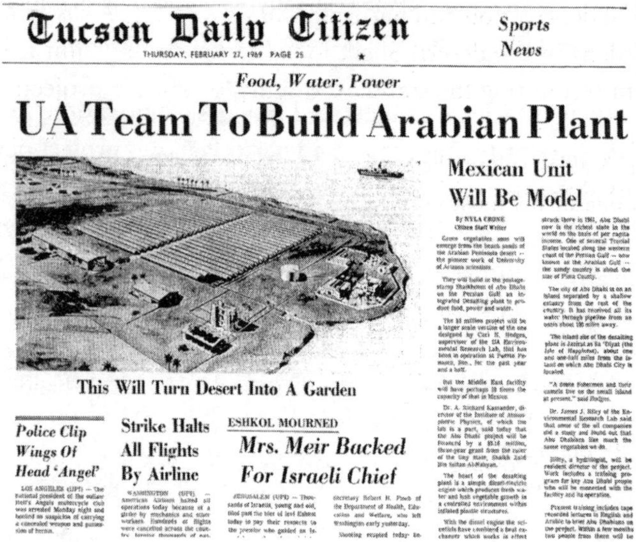

Tucson Daily Citizen

THURSDAY, FEBRUARY 27, 1969 PAGE 25

Sports News

*Food, Water, Power*

# UA Team To Build Arabian Plant

This Will Turn Desert Into A Garden

## Mexican Unit Will Be Model

By NYLA CRONE
Citizen Staff Writer

Green vegetables soon will emerge from the beach sands of the Arabian Peninsula desert -- the pioneer work of University of Arizona scientists.

They will build in the postage-stamp Sheikhdom of Abu Dhabi on the Persian Gulf an integrated Desalting plant to produce food, power and water.

The $3 million project will be a larger scale version of the one designed by Carl N. Hodges, supervisor of the UA Environmental Research Lab, that has been in operation at Puerto Penasco, Son., for the past year and a half.

But the Middle East facility will have perhaps 10 times the capacity of that in Mexico.

Dr. A. Richard Kassander, director of the Institute of Atmospheric Physics, of which the lab is a part, said today that the Abu Dhabi project will be financed by a $3.16 million, three-year grant from the ruler of the tiny state, Shaikh Zaid Bin Sultan Al-Nahyan.

The heart of the desalting plant is a simple diesel-electric engine which produces fresh water and host vegetable growth in a controlled environment within inflated plastic structures.

With the diesel engine the scientists have combined a heat exchanger which works in effect

struck there in 1961, Abu Dhabi now is the richest state in the world on the basis of per capita income. One of several Trucial States located along the western coast of the Persian Gulf -- now known as the Arabian Gulf -- the sandy country is about the size of Pima County.

The city of Abu Dhabi is on an island separated by a shallow estuary from the rest of the country. It has received all its water through pipeline from an oasis about 100 miles away.

The island site of the desalting plant is Jazirat as Sa 'Diyat (the Isle of Happiness), about one and one-half miles from the island on which Abu Dhabi City is located.

"A dozen fishermen and their camels live on the small island at present," said Hodges.

Dr. James J. Riley of the Environmental Research Lab said that some of the oil companies did a study and found out that Abu Dhabians like much the same vegetables we do.

Riley, a hydrologist, will be resident director of the project. Work includes a training program for key Abu Dhabi people who will be connected with the facility and its operation.

Present training includes tape recorded lectures in English and Arabic to brief Abu Dhabians on the project. Within a few months two people from there will be

*Police Clip Wings Of Head 'Angel'*

LOS ANGELES (UPI) — The national president of the outlaw Hell's Angels motorcycle club was arrested Monday night and booked on suspicion of carrying a concealed weapon and possession of heroin.

Strike Halts All Flights By Airline

WASHINGTON (UPI) — American Airlines halted all operations today because of a strike by mechanics and other workers. Hundreds of flights were canceled across the country, leaving thousands of ...

ESHKOL MOURNED

*Mrs. Meir Backed For Israeli Chief*

JERUSALEM (UPI) — Thousands of Israelis, young and old, filed past the bier of Levi Eshkol today to pay their respects to the premier who guided ...

secretary Robert H. Finch of the Department of Health, Education and Welfare, who left Washington early yesterday.

Shooting erupted today ...

***Figure* 4.3.** Tucson Daily Citizen *breaking the news about the ERL project in Abu Dhabi.*

In early 1969, news broke that the UA Environmental Research Laboratory was being commissioned to build a cutting-edge combined greenhouse-desalination facility in Abu Dhabi, which researchers had piloted in the Mexican town of Puerto Peñasco. It was announced in a front-page story in the *Tucson Daily Citizen,* accompanied by an image proclaiming that the project would turn the "desert into a garden."[21] The basic idea of the Abu Dhabi project was to follow the Puerto Peñasco prototype and use small, diesel-powered desal machines to generate water for an array of plastic-covered greenhouses. By today's standards, the project may not seem cutting-edge, but this was the beginning of what is now known as "controlled-environment agriculture," encompassing hydroponics, aquaponics, vertical farming, and more.

The US media coverage of the ERL project in Abu Dhabi was sensational and exoticizing, especially in the way that reporters fixated on Sheikh Zayed's impressive wealth in a land of deprivation and hardship. A *Los Angeles Times* article, "Gardens in the desert: Sheik looks to the future," illustrates this in recounting the standard origin story of the project:

> An Arabian sultan, the Sheik of Abu Dhabi, believes the answer to one of his most perplexing problems lies on the beach of Puerto Peñasco, a remote Mexican fishing village. What particularly annoys Sheik Zaid Bin Sultan Al-Nahyan, ruler of a postage-stamp sized Persian Gulf Principality, is the price of fresh vegetables in his oil-rich country. Abu Dhabians pay $1.50 a pound for vegetables flown to their sand hills from Lebanon. The Sheik is fascinated with an inexpensive, revolutionary process of growing food on coastal desert lands developed in recent months in the Mexican village on the northeastern shores of the Gulf of California. It's a complicated system, simple to operate, that utilizes distilled sea water, polyethylene "greenhouses," waste energy from small diesel engines and "scrubbed" smog (Carbon Dioxide).
>
> When the Sheik heard about the successful experiment in Puerto Peñasco he dashed off a check for $3.16 million to build a similar project in his desert kingdom large enough to keep his 50,000 subjects in fresh vegetables year round. The check went to the University of Arizona Environmental Research Laboratory here—inventors of the combined system that provides cheap power, water and food on desert coastal lands. Carl N. Hodges, 32, director of the laboratory, on a recent world trip to places potentially suitable for the process, visited Abu Dhabi. Hodges said it was possible for Abu Dhabi to produce two million pounds of high-quality vegetables a year on its sand dunes at a cost of less than 10 cents a pound.[22]

The *L.A. Times* report went on to characterize Abu Dhabi as "the richest nation on earth per capita" thanks to a "fantastic oil boom." Other news outlets stressed Zayed's spectacular wealth, but also described him as a transformative leader, ready to join the American vision of modernity. The *San Francisco Chronicle*, for example, described his emirate as the "remote Sheikhdom of Abu Dhabi—one of the virtually unknown trucial states," and the ruler himself as being intent on "speeding his nation into the world of Now. A decade ago Abu Dhabi had nothing—sand, a dusty port, a couple of inland oases where dates and a few vegetables grew. Now there is oil, vast reservoirs of it, and oil royalties are pouring into the Sheikhdom, spurring schools, roads, and a modern style"—and, the author adds, a UA-built "self-powered food factory."[23] Illustrating the US government's active support for the ERL project, the State Department sent this article to all of the science attachés and science officers at embassies in the Middle East, North Africa, and South Asia.[24]

Most accounts of the ERL project highlighted Zayed's ability to allocate large sums of money on a whim, and framing him as an "Arabian sultan" and the ruler of a fantastically wealthy "postage-stamp Shaikhdom [...] now is the richest state in the world."[25] In true Orientalist fashion, a sense of awe and surprise permeates the articles, as they dwell on the titillating possibilities of collaborating with a leader who can so easily write a check for what might be otherwise deemed a risky investment on the part of the UA: "Kassander said the small, oil-rich nation, whose 50,000 Arab residents are mostly illiterate, sent the university enough money to finance the building of the desalting plant with the balance deposited in Abu Dhabi banks to be spent there for on-site construction."[26] Such demeaning characterizations of local Arabs as "illiterate" or otherwise backward were so frequent in the reporting that it was obviously a point of pride—evidence of Zayed's unique desire to modernize his territory through partnering with the high-tech visionaries of the University of Arizona.

The media drew heavily from the familiar tropes of "backwardness" and "modernity" common to imperial visions the world over, and these stereotypes were clearly useful for Carl Hodges too. He and his partners at the University of Arizona tapped into these fantasies to position the ERL project as a kind of international charity—spreading the modernizing lessons of America's arid empire to other corners of the globe. In the ERL's imperial understanding of Sheikh Zayed and his "illiterate" populace, they had money and resources under their feet, but they lacked the expertise to harness it. They couldn't even grow their own food, as a *Tucson Daily Citizen* article suggested: "Take one tiny Saudi Arabian sheikdom of sand, sea and sun, mix in some scientific expertise from the University of Arizona and what do you have? Vegetables sprouting from the desert—tomatoes, cucumbers, squash, lettuce, eggplant, peppers, broccoli and cabbage."[27] In short, UA's arid lands experts can make the desert bloom!

The ERL's Abu Dhabi project was yet another iteration of the arid empire narratives that have circulated between Arizona and Arabian deserts for decades: the modernizers will come with their farming skills and cultivate modernity. And yet this vision of arid empire was also specific to the Cold War moment. The project fit neatly into the optimistic narratives of the Green Revolution, which framed new agricultural technologies as silver-bullet solutions to famine and poverty on the one hand, and a preemptive measure to stave off the threat of communist revolution on the other.[28] That is, if US-backed agricultural innovation could feed the masses in poor but newly independent countries, those masses would be less susceptible to the Soviet Union's efforts to provoke communist revolution. Or so the story went.

By tapping into this Cold War narrative, the ERL promised to build a real-world model of the techno-optimist future the US-led capitalist bloc was selling to newly independent countries. Building on the rhetoric of wonderment associated with the Green Revolution, newspaper headlines underscored the element of surprise in the UA's extraordinary reach to the deserts of Arabia: "It can be done in a sand dune," "From the big greenhouse in Tucson to the sands of Abu Dhabi," "lush fruit growing in sand signals wasteland conquest."[29] Here, the Green Revolution was imagined to *conquer* the most challenging of environments—desert "wastelands." Cold War anxieties gave special salience to the ERL project, but it remained part of the same vision of arid empire that had bound Arizona and Arabia for decades.

If Arizona's experts were out to conquer the deserts of distant lands with their high-tech agricultural innovations, the rulers of those places also had a role to play in the theater of arid empire. As noted already, there was no commercial agriculture to speak of in the Trucial States in the 1960s. Beyond some date farming and small-scale oasis production, Abu Dhabi was still dominated by sand dunes and saw no benefits from the British Digdagga Agricultural Trials Station in the northern emirate of Ras Al-Khaimah. This situation frustrated Abu Dhabi's emir, Sheikh Zayed bin Sultan Al Nahyan, who keenly understood the symbolic power of promoting agriculture and all kinds of desert greening projects.[30] Zayed had deposed his elder brother, Sheikh Shakhbut, as ruler of Abu Dhabi in 1966, in large part because Shakhbut was notoriously stingy and refused to use revenue from oil, discovered in 1958, for the territory's development.

Zayed's dream of modernizing Abu Dhabi was the basis of his claims to be the emirate's legitimate ruler, and he wasted no time in adopting policies and allocating funds to promote development. Modernizing the emirate's food supply and bringing green vegetation to the desert landscape was a fundamental part of this vision. Desert greening projects were so important, in fact, that they would eventually ossify into a core tenet of Emirati nationalism under his developmentalist promise of "Zayedism." In line with Western constructions of desert landscapes as somehow inferior or deficient, Zayed's vision hinged on a "cultural valuation of the green environment as better than the 'natural' dry desert."[31]

In this negative framing, the desert's barrenness was thus approached as a problem that required intervention from a benevolent leader. The spectacle of conquering nature and "rolling back the desert" allowed Zayed to evince his compassionate care for his people and his land. The ERL project thus helped him advance this image of benevolence, as well as demonstrating his ability to entice prestigious international cooperation. But Zayed's developmentalist messages did not circulate on their own: individuals had to broadcast them. Here he found an eager ally in Carl Hodges—a man who shared his passion for greening the desert and self-aggrandizement, and who would become a strategic ally just like Karl Twitchell had been for King Ibn Saud decades before.

In all the fanfare that Hodges received from the international media for his desert "food factory," he tended to be cast as the leading hero—not just because he was ERL's supervisor, but because he was an "evangelist" for making deserts bloom through high-tech solutions to climate and resource limitations. He claimed to despise the cliché of "making the desert bloom," but it nonetheless served his purposes well as it helped him sell his laboratory's techno-optimistic visions of high-tech food and water solutions for coastal deserts.[32] For him, the Abu Dhabi project was no less than a "cornucopian transformation" of a "parched islet off the Arabian mainland":

> There, desalted seawater, distilled with waste heat captured from generators, is used to irrigate vegetables inside plastic-skinned greenhouses in which the microclimate can be regulated. All of this may seem reminiscent of *Dune*, a 1967 Frank Herbert novel that ecology buffs have evangelized as almost a new *Book of Revelations*. In *Dune* the locale is a waterless planet bereft of any verdure save that in an indoor garden. In Abu Dhabi the nonfictional indoor gardens promote fertility where dust

storms, heat, and aridity preclude ordinary agriculture, and the low, sparse shrubs barely sustain a few browsing camels.[33]

It is no coincidence that Hodges references Frank Herbert's *Dune*, since this sci-fi novel stood at the center of a growing set of conversations in the United States about environmental catastrophe, as we will see in the next chapter. It was this promise of a fantastic "cornucopian transformation" in the barren desert that Hodges was selling Sheikh Zayed.

Not everyone was so convinced, however. A few murmurs about the unreasonable cost of the project surfaced on occasion, including one article in *The Times* of London. Citing the millions of dollars already invested, *The Times* described the project as "a typical example of reversing nature and proving that the desert can be made fertile—but at considerable cost."[34] An academic evaluation later highlighted the fact that the project depended on oil-based inputs, including energy, water, and capital, showing merely that "virtually anything can be produced if cost is ignored."[35] The ERL project was supposed to solve the Arabian Peninsula's food problem, often encapsulated by the refrain, "we can't eat oil"—but in actual fact, Hodges's scheme would entrench the region's reliance on oil to power the desal plants. Or, as one reporter pointed out in an early story about the ERL's mission in Abu Dhabi: "Actually, all this horticulture is more show biz than science right now."[36]

Carl Hodges was a major force behind the "show biz" character of the UA's scheme in Abu Dhabi. But Sheikh Zayed and his supporters were also interested in promoting the spectacle of the high-tech greenhouse. In a December 1968 letter outlining the agreement between the University of Arizona and Abu Dhabi's leaders, Emirati representative Sayed M.H. Juma explained their support for the greenhouse project:

> It is our hope that Abu Dhabi can set an example of the desirability of using government resources for progressive development

of our arid lands. I am well aware that the University of Arizona is a world leader in the area of arid lands research, and would very much like to have this project integrated into the total arid lands research and development project of the University of Arizona.[37]

This letter came less than a year after the British announcement in January 1968 that they would be ending the Trucial States protectorate agreements. Zayed was angling to take the helm of the newly independent country – what was to become the United Arab Emirates – following their withdrawal in December 1971. Inviting the ERL to set up the facility in Abu Dhabi right at this moment was an important way for Zayed to show that he could deliver on his promise to modernize the Emirati food system, green the desert, and build strategic international partnerships.

The ERL desalination and greenhouse project was ultimately realized, and fresh produce, primarily tomatoes and cucumbers, started to grow in the Abu Dhabi desert. The greenhouses may have been one project among Zayed's many diverse efforts to showcase his fitness to lead an independent UAE, but it was a spectacular one. Judging from the parade of visiting dignitaries brought to tour it, including countless world leaders, the boxer Muhammad Ali, and others, it served his interests well—but only for a relatively short time.

The ERL–Abu Dhabi partnership was consistently rocky, and by 1974, the University of Arizona withdrew completely. The diesel-powered desalination components were relocated elsewhere on Abu Dhabi's coast, while the greenhouses were dismantled and sent to the interior town of Al-Ain, long a stronghold of the UAE's small but influential agricultural community. There is no official account of why the project ended, but combined with the UAE's shifting priorities after independence in 1971, a series of convoluted interpersonal and political disagreements between Hodges and Sheikh Zayed, University of Arizona officials, and the US Department of State all contributed to the initiative's ultimate demise.

Despite the seductive media storyline about the millions of dollars flowing freely from the Arabian sands, the financial and political relationship between the Emirati and American partners was fraught from the start. Shortly after the project got off the ground, Sheikh Zayed toured the ERL's greenhouse facilities on Abu Dhabi's Saadiyat Island on July 23, 1970. During this visit, Hodges apparently invited Zayed and/or his son to visit the United States for a "scientific tour," which would cover facilities in Arizona, the University of Arizona facility at Puerto Peñasco, and Hawaii.[38] Hodges also thought a visit to New York City and Washington, DC, would be in order. For Sheikh Zayed, such a visit to the United States would have been a political coup: it would leave no question as to his rightful claim to the leadership of the Trucial States following the British withdrawal. He and his advisers pushed hard to make it happen.

Several weeks after Zayed visited the ERL facilities, Hodges met with representatives from the State Department to discuss the logistics of arranging an official state visit. Since the UAE was not yet independent, Zayed was still only the Emir of Abu Dhabi, a British protectorate, *not* the leader of a sovereign state. Hodges recognized that this complicated matters, but he pointed out to State Department officials "that Shaykh Zayid had already made 'state visits' to Beirut, Amman and Rawalpindi."[39] The ruler of Bahrain had also recently visited the US for an official visit in 1969, before that territory became independent in 1971, and so it was not wholly unreasonable to assume that Zayed might be given similar consideration. Hodges's lobbying efforts, however, were ignored by the State Department officials.

Hodges started to get frantic and next turned to Arizona State Senator, Paul J. Fannin. In a letter to Fannin dated

September 28, 1970, Hodges made his case for inviting Zayed to the United States, explaining to the senator that "it would be extremely desirable (as a matter of fact critical to the success of our long-range objectives, I believe) for His Highness to visit the United States and take a scientific tour of various projects here. In that way, he can better understand the benefits of his commitments to research, development and training."[40] He also made sure the senator understood that Zayed was not just a benevolent leader but destined to become the supreme leader upon decolonization, making Zayed's allegiance politically significant for advancing US interests in the region when the British left the Trucial States:

> I know, from my meetings with Shaikh Zayed, that he is an outstanding individual. He honestly has the welfare of the people of Abu Dhabi as his main concern. Unfortunately, he is under tremendous pressures to budget a greater and greater portion of his wealth for military purchases and other such activities. He must justify any commitment he makes to research, development and training in terms of well-defined future benefits. I believe Shaikh Zayed will become the Ruler of the Federation of Trucial States when it is finally formed, and, as such, will be a most powerful figure in the Persian Gulf. With this consideration, it is not only of great importance to the University of Arizona that he come to the United States under favorable conditions, but of significance, I believe, to the whole United States.

In this letter to Fannin, Hodges acknowledged that the visit he was requesting for Sheikh Zayed would probably need to be private. He was nonetheless explicitly requesting the senator's help with getting an invitation from President Nixon and perhaps some kind of audience in Washington:

> Because of the political situation in the Arab world, it is probably desirable that His Highness's visit be a private one, with

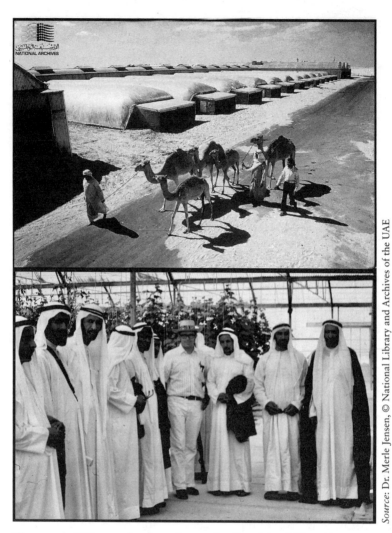

*Figure 4.4.* ERL greenhouse project on Saadiyat Island. Top: Air supported greenhouses covered with polyethylene plastic, viewed from outside. Bottom: Arid Lands Research Center Director Dr. James Riley (center) provides a tour of the Saadiyat program to Sheikh Zayed Bin Sultan Al Nahyan (second from right) and Sheikh Rashid Bin Saeed Al Maktoum (right).

***Figure 4.5.*** ERL greenhouse project on Saadiyat Island. Top: The first University of Arizona team with the Abu Dhabi trainees on Saadiyat Island, left to right: Miguel Fontes, Omar Baki, Dr. John O'Toole, Hamad Tamin, Dr. Hamdi Qafishheh, Abdulla Kaddas, Dr. James J. Riley and Mohammed Mijrin Seif. Sign reads: "Established for the people of Abu Dhabi through a grant from H H Shaikh Zayid bin Sultan al Niyan to the University of Arizona." Bottom: Tomato variety "Tropi-Red" developed in the state of Florida, USA and grown on Saadiyat Island, Abu Dhabi as part of the University of Arizona Research Project.

the University of Arizona as host; that would eliminate the possible political criticism of his visit. I know, however, that he is extremely impressed with the international activities of the United States in all areas and would be particularly pleased to receive some comments from President Nixon regarding his visit—and, of course, honored if he might have an invitation to at least visit, briefly and informally, with the President. I have, therefore, prepared the enclosed suggested draft letter that President Nixon might consider sending to Shaikh Zayed. Could I ask your assistance in presenting this suggested letter to the President and requesting his cooperation?

The suggested draft letter from Nixon in **Figure 4.6** is what Hodges included with his letter to Senator Fannin. In line with the US's post-war involvement in academia to extend its imperial reach, Hodges here moved fluidly from the narrow role of scientific adviser and into the realm of diplomacy. Hodges was not just confident that "Zayed will become the Ruler of the Federation of Trucial States" (or the United Arab Emirates, as it came to be named)—he was actually *helping* Zayed to solidify this position as the "natural" leader of the soon-to-be independent country.

The audacity of writing in the name of the US president is itself remarkable, but Hodges's references to the desert environments in his draft letter to Nixon are also important. He praises Zayed's commitment to cooperating through R&D in "man's last great reserve, the deserts of the world," here conjuring arid lands as a geopolitical conduit of exchange. Hodges also tries to pull in the landscape connection by noting that Nixon was raised in the US Southwest—Yorba Linda, California, to be precise.

Nixon's hometown, now part of the sprawling Los Angeles megalopolis, differs in countless ways from Arizona's Sonoran desert and Abu Dhabi's Arabian desert. But in Hodges's letter, the "desert" and the "Southwest" do a very particular kind

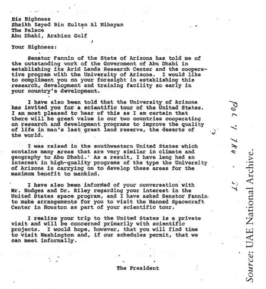

Draft of suggested letter for
President Nixon to His Highness
Shaikh Zayed Bin Sultan Al Nihayan

His Highness
Shaikh Zayed Bin Sultan Al Nihayan
The Palace
Abu Dhabi, Arabian Gulf

Your Highness:

Senator Fannin of the State of Arizona has told me of
the outstanding work of the Government of Abu Dhabi in
establishing its Arid Lands Research Center and the cooperative program with the University of Arizona. I would like
to compliment you on your foresight in establishing this
research, development and training facility so early in
your country's development.

I have also been told that the University of Arizona
has invited you for a scientific tour of the United States.
I am most pleased to hear of this as I am certain that
there will be great value in our two countries cooperating
on research and development programs to improve the quality
of life in man's last great land reserve, the deserts of
the world.

I was raised in the southwestern United States which
contains many areas that are very similar in climate and
geography to Abu Dhabi.' As a result, I have long had an
interest in high-quality programs of the type the University
of Arizona is carrying on to develop these areas for the
maximum benefit to mankind.

I have also been informed of your conversation with
Mr. Hodges and Dr. Riley regarding your interest in the
United States space program, and I have asked Senator Fannin
to make arrangements for you to visit the Manned Spacecraft
Center in Houston as part of your scientific tour.

I realize your trip to the United States is a private
visit and will be concerned primarily with scientific
projects. I would hope, however, that you will find time
to visit Washington and, if our schedules permit, that we
can meet informally.

The President

*Source: UAE National Archive.*

*Figure 4.6.* Draft letter that Hodges wrote in the name of President
Nixon, appended to his letter to Senator Fannin, September 1970.

of work: they are a rhetorical bridge uniting Nixon, the US
government, Sheikh Zayed, and the future state that Zayed
would lead. To dwell on the nuances of physical geography
would undercut the utility of the desert as a story of connection between Arizona and Abu Dhabi. In this way, Hodges was
a fluent agent of arid empire, advancing US influence overseas
while also advancing Zayed's aspirations of taking control of
an independent UAE. That is, he tried.

Unfortunately for Carl Hodges, there were greater forces con-
straining his efforts to woo Sheikh Zayed and to make good
on his promise of securing a visit to America for the aspiring
leader. US officials ultimately refused to issue an invitation.
Zayed had watched the royal families of his neighbors in Saudi
Arabia and Bahrain get the stately treatment in America in

years prior, and he clearly felt entitled to it himself. The British and other foreign governments also had begun to host him as the leader of the Trucial States. So when the US government balked, the issue escalated beyond an injured ego; it became entangled with the Arizona project financing. At some point in the fall of 1970, at the same time that Hodges was trying (and failing) to arrange Zayed's official visit, the Emirati leader started to walk back his financial promises to the University of Arizona.

Hodges then began pressing different government agencies for financial support for the ERL project, including USAID. According to one State Department memo, USAID declined to contribute funding in November 1970 because the "project failed meet criteria of AID legislation, i.e. Abu Dhabi meets none of financial qualifications of an underdeveloped nation." Hodges was not pleased and apparently neither was Sheikh Zayed. Hodges telephoned State Department officials to tell them that the rejection "greatly disturbed Ruler Abu Dhabi who feels our position has political implications reflecting adversely on him personally. Ruler apparently has suggested our position reflective of USG disinterest in Arabs generally."[41] This led Zayed to then refuse "to release to University Arizona promised counterpart funds and even to furnish sum equivalent to preliminary commitment."[42] As a result of the USAID rejection, Hodges told officials that the financial situation was "critical" and if Zayed failed to "release funds this will put serious crimp in Arizona University budget and quite possibly lead to closing down of project."[43]

The situation became serious enough that both University of Arizona president Richard Harvill and Dick Kassander got involved and were communicating with the State Department officials in Dhahran. In one memo about a December 10 conversation between the parties, Harvill admits to having already misused university funds, extended "to support [the] project which it has no authorization to do."[44] Unsure of how to peacefully resolve the situation, the Arizona and State Department officials agreed that "nothing should be done to upset confidence on part Abu Dhabi leadership toward University personnel and project" and that the university would "take further risk on behalf this project." This meant that the UA leadership continued to misappropriate university funds for the UAE project and eventually secured several loans in the name of the Abu Dhabi Research Center (for $683,000 from First National City Bank in Arizona and $1.35 million from the Export-Import Bank of New York).[45]

The State Department staff was clearly frustrated by the debacle. An FYI appended to the December 1970 memo notes: "According to Hodges, who I feel is operating somewhat beyond his depth, Zayyid is also reportedly miffed that USG has not [...] invited him to visit United States."[46] Despite repeated efforts over the course of several years, I was never able to reach Hodges to hear his account of what happened, and he died in April 2021. I was able to interview some of the ERL staff who worked in Abu Dhabi in the 1970s, but the level of institutional malfeasance was so great and personal conflicts so severe that no one would go on the record discussing it, even fifty years later.

Although their individual testimonies on the matter are absent from the archival record, Sheikh Zayed probably *was* "miffed" and Hodges probably *was* "operating beyond his depth." Ultimately, each man was pursuing his own agenda while hoping the other would be the key to facilitating it. The only problem was that the US government was still uncertain of how to shape its imperial footprint in the Arabian Peninsula. When any officials weighed in, they wavered about how to treat the ruler of Abu Dhabi and, more generally, about how to approach the Trucial States' pending reconfiguration.

The American waffling partly reflected concerns around protocol. But it was ultimately tied to an issue of priority: US officials had closer ties with Saudi Arabia, and had already invested in a diffuse network of advocates there in the corporate, scientific, and political spheres. The Trucial States' status was ambiguous and the British were doing their own waffling about the shape of their future in the region.[47] Carl Hodges and his greenhouse project in Abu Dhabi were routinely stamped for attention by the Science officers within the State Department and, viewed from the desk of Senator Fannin or President Nixon (if his eyes even encountered the draft letter penned in his name), probably appeared as more of an annoyance than an exciting prospect for cooperation in a region where future allegiances were already being defined by Aramco and the deep ties that had been developing in Saudi Arabia since the 1940s.

The entire ordeal eventually reached a peaceful settlement, although Sheikh Zayed never got his much hoped-for official visit to the US. In July 1972, Harvill stepped down as University of Arizona president and was replaced by John Schaefer. In Schaefer's first correspondence with the Emirati partners, two weeks after assuming his post, he wrote to express "deep regret" that he had "inherited some misunderstandings." Hoping to "remove any possible tension between us," he set out a financial and logistical plan for the remainder of 1971 and noted in closing, "We would welcome the discussions of a new technical assistance contract with Abu Dhabi commencing January 1, 1972 because we believe the similarity of the climatic conditions of our two states make our association a potentially beneficial one."[48] In smoothing ruffled feathers, Schaefer returned to the desert as bridge. This geopolitical narrative built on arid empire's story of commonality worked for a time, but as with the other entanglements between Arizona and Arabia, direct points of connection were easily undone even if the broader logic remained.

Financial and diplomatic tussles aside, the ERL project in Abu Dhabi met with many successes. The desalination machines were an exciting advance that foreshadowed the possibility for desal-enabled growth across the Arabian Peninsula. The greenhouses also grew impressive amounts of gleaming vegetables out of the sand dunes. Yet the productiveness of the greenhouses ended up becoming a problem for University of Arizona leaders, since they wanted to use the project to boast about their *scientific* advances. Simply continuing to grow large amounts of fruits and vegetables lost its luster once it was proven to be possible. Faced with this reality, Hodges became increasingly agitated by what he saw as the lack of Emirati commitment to research.

A 1972 fire at the greenhouse damaged the facility's research office, but the Emirati partners long neglected to rebuild it as they had promised.[49] In a 1973 letter to Sheikh Hadif bin Humaid of the Abu Dhabi government's Sadiyat Committee, Hodges complained bitterly about the situation. His letter explained that, as much as he wanted the University of Arizona to remain in Abu Dhabi, "it is now time for the Government to make a fundamental decision as to whether they wish the Sadiyat project to run strictly as a vegetable production facility or if they wish a continued cooperative research effort between the Government of Abu Dhabi and the University of Arizona." He continued:

> If the Government wishes to deemphasize research and development and simply operate Sadiyat during 1974 for the production of vegetables, the University of Arizona should no longer be involved with the Technical Assistance Agreement. We have a great number of requests for research and development projects to be directed by our staff, and our talents can be more effectively utilized as research scientists than as simply vegetable production advisors. If, on the other hand, the Government of Abu Dhabi wishes to carry on the outstanding research and development effort they have initiated on Sadiyat, the University wants to be part of that effort.[50]

In essence, Hodges did not feel that his team was doing enough science to justify their continued work at the Arizona-run greenhouses. Hodges was known for his temper, and the tone he strikes in this letter is telling—trying to perform some gestures of respect, but ultimately belying his anger that UA's credentialed researchers should be treated as mere "vegetable production advisors."

Ironically, the showbiz master himself was confounded by the Emirati partners' interest in a different kind of showbiz. For them, the modern greenhouses were primarily an icon of Sheikh Zayed's paternal care for the population and his ability to bring in foreigners to develop the country. The university's research agenda was essentially irrelevant. Yet even Zayed's use of the ERL project as a developmentalist spectacle faded quickly. Once the UAE became an independent state in 1971, he was able to reap the rewards of its expanding oil exports, and local perceptions of "modernity" began to rapidly shift. Within a few short years, the ERL's greenhouses were no longer in line with the government's vision for modern development on Saadiyat—the island now being targeted as a special enclave for the capital's elites. Arizona's icon of high-tech desert farming was destined to be forgotten.

When Sheikh Zayed had originally commissioned the UA project, he was focused on rural development. With independence and oil wealth, however, his vision for Abu Dhabi's future was as a glimmering capital city. The political calculus of Zayed's own arid empire had changed: now the desalinated seawater was going to flow to sparkling high-rises instead of greenhouses. These factors help explain why the UA project is not well known in the UAE today: quietly forgetting it returned Saadiyat to a *tabula rasa*, while not tarnishing Zayed's paternalist image.[51] Reimagining Saadiyat as empty, undeveloped land was a successful tactic. Very few people know the history of the University of Arizona's project and instead, the island is now known for its new, ultra-elite icons of modernity. The site where the greenhouses once stood is now occupied by Abu Dhabi's new Louvre Museum, designed by Jean Nouvel and opened in 2017. Just around the corner, a Frank Gehry–designed Guggenheim is set to open in 2025.

The University of Arizona's greenhouse project in the desert may have been brushed aside, but it is indicative of how US agents of empire worked through scientific networks built around arid lands expertise to promote their visions of modernity —not just in the desert Southwest, but, increasingly, overseas. From the case of Middle Eastern date palms in the Arizona desert to the Arizona farmers at work in Saudi Arabia and the Trucial States, the desert became a site of *opportunity* for these actors, their own scientific laboratory. Just like the arid empire that white settlers built in Arizona, Arabia afforded another kind of "empty" space to build one's credentials through dryland agriculture and arid lands science.

The ERL's Abu Dhabi project also reflects how those working in the name of arid lands science were seldom driven by a "pure" intellectual motive. Rather, as with any other kind of labor, the work that individuals invested in "making the desert bloom" was fueled by overlapping financial, political, and personal motivations. As America's arid empire became a model overseas, the tenuous first steps of Arizona's researchers in Abu Dhabi clearly privileged the same people who were privileged in settling Arizona: entrepreneurial white males like Carl Hodges, Dick Kassander, and the UA presidents Richard Harvill and Jack Schaefer.

These men all worked together to entrench the university's role in the increasingly entrepreneurial US academy of the 1960s and '70s.[52] In angling for large external grants to fill university coffers, they learned that their desert story was a powerful one. Hodges's effort to bring Arizona dryland expertise to the UAE came in part from working with Kassander to bring in big-money grants for the university. Kassander, who would later become UA's first vice president of research, found Hodges to be a useful tool in selling the University of Arizona's arid lands expertise: Hodges did not push for the Emirati project because it was expected of him but because he took great pride in his ability to sell his desert visions to well-endowed foundations and "Arabian sultans" alike. For Kassander, it was helpful that his beloved protégé liked the financial rewards and the political associations just as much as he liked the science.

The desert served as a kind of glue binding together his projects in Arizona and the Arabian Peninsula—indeterminate but eminently useful when fused with the jubilant spirit of Cold War techno-optimism and decolonization. UA staffers and their Emirati partners were joining forces around a desert story at a moment of shifting imperial relations in the Arabian Peninsula. They were navigating the rise of new states in 1971, the retreat or realignment of British colonial institutions and actors, and the rise of new American technocratic and capitalist forms of imperialism. But they were also part of *creating* this new political geography of independent states, using the tools of arid empire to bolster this shifting territoriality of power, as well as their own personal agendas.

The ERL project certainly didn't stand alone in legitimating Sheikh Zayed's ultimate claim to be the leader of the UAE upon independence. But it did bolster his effort to present himself as a modern and benevolent father figure invested in the good of his people, and as a leader esteemed by the international community. Crucially, in the intertwining of the political lives of Sheikh Zayed and Carl Hodges, and their allies (or opponents) in the bureaucracies of the University of Arizona and the US government, the desert became a strategic site to both facilitate and justify political, financial, and scientific flows and exchange between Arizona and the Arabian Peninsula. For them, the "desert" was a valuable resource to realize their goals.

Arid empire is unequivocally a story of science and expertise because of how researchers transcend borders through their technologies, ideas, and networks. Yet these exchanges need not count as successes to be relevant; failures matter too. The partnership didn't work precisely as Hodges or Zayed wished, but failed projects have afterlives. Since 2019, the Emirati government has been pumping hundreds of millions of dollars into new "AgTech" initiatives to promote modern greenhouse projects in the country.[53] As with the ERL project in the 1960s and '70s, today's AgTech projects traffic in the same kinds of images and stories about taming the desert through a techno-fetishistic modernity—all while forgetting the failure of the same visions during the heyday of Cold War modernization schemes. The Cold War ended decades ago, but the continuation of America's informal empire through the networks of science, technology, and higher education is still with us today.

The diverse high-tech agricultural projects in the UAE illustrate how arid empire has been built and sustained through these networks of science and expertise. And they show how it continues to hinge on earlier ways of imagining the desert not just as a barren "wasteland," but also as a place in need of intervention to be tamed and made productive. These interventions are imperial insofar as they take control of the land and organize people around an expert's view of order and civilization. When salesmen like Hodges or Zayed define the shape of these imperial interventions in the desert, they also define their own significance as "visionaries" and naturalize their role as leaders. The desert provides an especially useful foil for the drama and impressiveness of their alleged achievements in the most harrowing, inclement, exotic, uncivilized, or otherwise oppositional settings.

The Cold War moment charged this narrative with high-stakes political drama and, crucially, the financial and institutional support to bring the theater to life. By tapping into these symbolic and material resources to build a futuristic model of Arizona expertise applied to Arabian sands, the ERL project reworked arid empire's vision of bounty and capitalist expansion through the new language of techno-optimism and engineering ingenuity to defy all threats of resource scarcity in the desert.

Extravagant schemes to "make the desert bloom" are, unfortunately, always built on unsustainable patterns of using water and energy. Hodges's grand dream of solar-powered desal was supposed to overcome this problem, but it failed then and remains far-off today. Yet Hodges's project in Abu Dhabi showed that spectacle could help the public ignore the shortcomings of desal-enabled development in the Arabian Peninsula. In this sense, he furthered the American project of hiding the inequalities of arid empire, environmental violence, and intergenerational injustice. The disorienting invisibility of arid empire is not just limited to past and present, though. As we see in the next chapter, it includes the future too.

# 5

# Dreams

*In which we chase the apocalyptic imagination
of arid imperialists through sci-fi dreams of
colonizing extraterrestrial desert landscapes,
which were both imagined and realized in
Arizona and Arabia since the 1960s.*

Not long after the University of Arizona officially took leave
of its desal-greenhouse project in Abu Dhabi, the Environmental Research Laboratory got involved in developing another
experimental facility, this time back in Arizona. "Biosphere 2"
was a sprawling complex supposed to recreate the conditions
of Biosphere 1 (Earth) as a closed system. It was essentially
an oversized greenhouse of hypermodern geodesic domes and
glass panes covering a 3.14-acre floor area. The world is now
populated with countless flashy eco-centric design projects
and iconic laboratories, but when Biosphere 2 was initially
conceived in the mid-1980s, it was wholly new.

Biosphere 2 was equipped with a special sealed air system,
with the idea that researchers could be locked inside for several
years to test their ability to maintain the ecosystem that kept
them alive. At least, it was supposed to: after two failed trials in
the 1990s, the closed system experiment was deemed a failure.
Design woes notwithstanding, Biosphere 2's supposed contribution to the world of science was relayed to the public through
an apocalyptic story of looming environmental catastrophe,

*Source:* Author, December 2019.

*Figure 5.1. View of the Biosphere 2 facilities in Oracle, Arizona.*

which would require humanity to move off-planet. Biosphere 2 marked a shift in arid empire's logic, which settler scientists had earlier applied to the immediate demands of colonization in the Arizona desert. Now it was to be harnessed in preparation for the colonization of desert landscapes on other planets.

Preparing for interstellar existence was always a stated goal of the Biosphere 2 project, and its originators constantly emphasized the need to "get ready" for the impending environmental collapse of Earth. John Allen and Mark Nelson, two of the men behind the project, wrote in their conceptual tract, *Space Biospheres*, that humanity had a "historic imperative" to colonize territories beyond Earth: "biospherics opens up, together with astronautics, the ecotechnical possibilities, even the historic imperative, to expand Earth-life into the solar system and beyond that to the stars and then in time's good opportunity to the galaxies."[1] Allen and Nelson claimed that extraterrestrial colonization would be possible by 1995 and, though they were far off the mark with the timeline, the fanciful Biosphere 2 project is yet another iteration of arid empire's development, through the language and logics of modern techno-science. And it too sits at the intersection of scientific exchange and romantic stories about the deserts of Arizona and Arabia.

In the way that Cold War modernization schemes joined with arid lands science in the ERL project in Abu Dhabi, Biosphere 2 was conceived from arid empire's fusion with newly articulated visions of eco-catastrophism that emerged in the 1960s and gathered strength in the following decades. Doomsday narratives about the world's impending environmental collapse are commonplace in contemporary discussions about climate change, but Americans have been avidly reading these stories for decades.

Apocalyptic stories of environmental catastrophe were launched into mainstream discourse in the US and other Western countries following the sensational release of Rachel Carson's *Silent Spring* in 1962 and Paul Ehrlich's *The Population Bomb* in 1968.[2] These books provoked widespread fear about ecological collapse and the future of humanity on planet Earth. At the time, some rejected the apocalyptic stories and began labeling their authors as overly pessimistic "doomsayers."[3] Yet these critics didn't necessarily reject the premise that environmental challenges were real and significant. Rather, they suggested, humanity just needed to double down on its greatest resource—ingenuity—to engineer new solutions to Earth's natural limits. These were the techno-optimists. One of the first advocates of this perspective was Alvin Toffler, whose 1970 book *Future Shock* reassured readers that geo-engineering and technology would avert the apocalypse.[4]

Toffler's book fueled a new way of thinking about environmental apocalypse. He and his fellow techno-optimists didn't reject the basic premise of the doomsaying eco-catastrophists: that humankind was consuming resources and polluting environments at such a rate that we were on a fast path for self-destruction. Rather, people like Toffler acknowledged this story and proposed a set of solutions rooted in science, engineering, computing, and spatial planning. In short, they co-opted the apocalypse to sell their optimistic technologies and social engineering schemes. Another word for these techno-optimists is "visioneers," a term coined by Patrick McCray to capture the hybrid nature of technological enthusiasts, who first imagine and then try to engineer radical new techno-futures.[5]

Speculators and dreamers by nature, visioneers inhabited a fringe place within the mainstream scientific establishment. But in places like the United States, where they have historically flourished, "their liminal research and propagandizing, existing on the threshold of respectability and academic visibility, can still exert a considerable pull on the public's imagination of the technological future."[6] Beginning in the 1970s, such visioneers united with various futurists and entrepreneurs to invite the public to imagine a world of environmental collapse (*the horror!*) where humans had to survive in an artificial environment of their own making, but where they had successfully harnessed modern technology and rose to the challenge (*the wonder!*).

Biosphere 2 was an exemplary case of this pseudo-scientific propagandizing. Nobody had ever thought to seal a bunch of humans in a glass bubble before Biosphere 2, but once we understand the history of arid empire, it becomes clear that such experimental projects in the desert are neither new nor progressive. Their logic is quintessentially colonial. As we have already seen, imperial projects are often positioned as benign "experiments" to introduce a new mode of social ordering. Biosphere 2 continues this very same tradition, including sitting at the intersection of both Arizona and Arabia's deserts. And here again, modernist science is valorized over other ways of knowing and helps to justify settler control of Indigenous lands. Biosphere 2 also featured the same hero

—the white male scientist, the visioneer—arriving just in time to save the day.

Biosphere 2 might be one of the best known examples of an eco-apocalypse-inspired project in the desert, but it was not the first. A similar project was designed in the Arizona desert just a few decades prior; named Arcosanti, it was the first experimental community in Arizona to pilot sustainable living, founded in 1970.

Arcosanti was the dream and life project of Paolo Soleri, an Italian-American architect who first came to Arizona as one of Frank Lloyd Wright's apprentices working on Wright's Taliesin West winter residence in Scottsdale. Soleri's approach to architecture and politics differed markedly from that of his famous teacher, but he likewise came to value the desert as a natural backdrop for selling his work. The young architect developed a conceptual approach to harmonizing architecture and the natural environment, which he called "arcology":

> In an arcology, the built environment and the living processes of the inhabitants interact as organs, tissues, and cells do in a highly evolved organism. This means that multiple systems work together, coordinated and integrated to minimize waste while maximizing efficient circulation of people and resources, employing multiuse structures, and exploiting solar orientation for lighting, heating, cooling, food production and esthetic impact.[7]

Arcology was Soleri's response to the environmental apocalypse narratives of the late 1960s. Cities needed to be developed vertically and designed as contained systems, rather than sprawling horizontally over the landscape. He illustrated this vision in a stunning text, *Arcology: The City in the Image of Man*, which includes extensive concept maps and diagrams, as well as massive city plans to showcase what arcology would mean in different settings.[8] Among the last of the example cities in the book is Arcosanti.

Arcosanti was the city plan selected to serve as the real-life prototype of Soleri's ideas in Arizona, and ground was broken in a remote location in the high desert north of Phoenix in 1970. Best described as a commune, Arcosanti was to run cooperatively and subsist primarily from the sale of its famous cast-metal bells—a money-making endeavor that Soleri started to fund the rest of the project. People still live and work in Arcosanti today, and when touring the site, visitors describe his influence as, in part, precolonial Middle Eastern towns. As one travel writer described it, "Arcosanti is a winding, pedestrian-oriented 'laboratory' [...] Its dome- and bubble-shaped buildings, pierced by cantilevered concrete slabs, appear to be influenced by, among other things, 1970s Modernism, sci-fi futurism, Italian hillside towns and Middle Eastern villages."[9]

Arcosanti's unusual architectural mixture of squares and circles was the inspiration for another futurist desert project by another kind of visioneer: Arcosanti directly influenced the landscape of the desert planet of Tatooine in George Lucas's *Star Wars* franchise.[10] One need not even visit Arcosanti to see the similarity: the visuals in *Arcology* immediately transport one to the *Star Wars* universe.[11] Soleri was not designing his communities with interstellar travel or settlement in mind, but his work evokes the futuristic aesthetic that many now associate with outer space, thanks primarily to the legacy of *Star Wars*. Indeed, Arcosanti still operates today, and its residents are referred to as "Arconauts."

Arcosanti's connection to outer-space thinking was not just the product of its *Star Wars* popularization. It actually fit within a dense web of texts, conversations, and visioneering arising from the story of environmental apocalypse and salvation that took off in the 1960s, an imagination fed by the era's science fiction novels. One of the touchstone texts in these

*Figure 5.2. View of Arcosanti from the community's café.*

circles was Frank Herbert's 1965 novel *Dune*, which eventually became one of the best-known and -loved sci-fi works of all time.[12] Herbert was himself part of this techno-enthusiast environmentalist community, building a home in Oregon that he described as an "ecological demonstration project," and at one point calling himself a "technopeasant."[13] Herbert's fascination with deserts and post-apocalyptic futures led *Dune* to become a key text in the constellation of ideas and influences that make up arid empire, ultimately linking techno-optimistic projects pioneered in the deserts of Arizona and Arabia.

*Dune* is set in the distant future and revolves around the story of a noble duke who is forced to relocate his family to a forbidding desert planet. The novel displays the themes of resource finitude that were prominent at the time of its publication by conjuring a world that must be abandoned when its natural environment has been stripped bare. Even though Herbert's book is a work of fiction, it joined Carson's *Silent Spring* and Ehrlich's *Population Bomb* as one of the

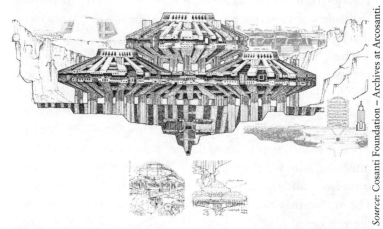

*Figure 5.3.* BABELDIGA *Dam Site, designed for a population of 1,200,000. Arcology Design from* Arcology – City in the Image of Man, *author Paolo Soleri, first edition by M.I.T. Press in 1970.*

most influential books for environmental activists in the late 1960s and 1970s. For the University of Arizona ERL supervisor, Carl Hodges, whom we met in the previous chapter, *Dune* was "a new Book of Revelations."[14] But *Dune* primarily appealed to the techno-optimists, who wanted to imagine that creative geo-engineering solutions could be harnessed to overcome the natural limitations of Earth and humanity. For his part, Hodges referenced the book's message of eco-apocalypse to justify the spectacular controlled environment projects that ERL was developing, including the Abu Dhabi facility and later, Biosphere 2 itself.

*Dune* had other Arabian connections too. In writing the book, Frank Herbert drew directly from famous texts about the Arabian desert by colonial explorers like T. E. Lawrence and Wilfred Thesiger, particularly with respect to their descriptions of local Bedouin tribes.[15] These British writers romanticized the desert as a hostile place where only the strong could survive and where non-locals had to adopt local customs to deal with hyper-arid conditions and extreme temperatures.

The desert, it was understood, was a place where the human challenges of surviving an austere, waterless world were most sharply posed.

The British travel writers that Herbert drew from also consistently depicted the desert as an utterly bizarre, alien space. The foreignness of the desert, its unearthly character, was central to *Dune*, as well. Like Arcosanti's unique architecture, what set *Dune* apart, the frightening but captivating story of a desert planet, was made still more popular by the *Star Wars* franchise. *Star Wars* is filled with "all manner of borrowings" from *Dune* and indeed, "Herbert knew he'd been ripped off."[16] The author may not have received due credit at the time, but the release of a new, highly anticipated *Dune* film directed by Denis Villeneuve in 2021 brought new awareness of this genealogy. Origin stories aside, *Dune* and *Star Wars* were both rooted in longstanding arid empire imaginaries in American popular culture that cast arid lands as foreign and dangerous. The films merely extended these tropes, now cementing the desert as an icon of apocalyptic, post-Earth futures. Desert planets inspired by Arabian sand dunes and an Arizona architectural commune: a fittingly arid combination for a story about (Galactic) Empire.

In expanding on the Western fantasy of human beings engineering their way out of eco-apocalypse, *Star Wars* and *Dune* also imply that *everyone* on Earth is headed for the apocalypse. Crucially, this storyline conceals the fact that huge portions of the world "have already lived through the ecological catastrophe brought about by European colonialism and its repercussions."[17] As Diné geographers Andrew Curley and Majerle Lister note, this history of dispossession has constituted its own "dystopia."[18] The past then combines with contemporary forms of marginalization to effect "multiple, overlapping, and current dystopias"—lived realities today, not some future fantasy of the sci-fi universe. For diverse

Indigenous communities, "the" apocalypse is both past and present.

Defining when and where the apocalypse occurs is an act of power. In the hands of techno-optimists and visioneers, nightmares of environmental crisis became a valuable commodity and an opportunity.[19] That is, if they could define the apocalypse, they could more easily sell their own solutions to engineer Earth and humanity out of its predicament. Here the Western scientist takes on a special prominence as a kind of "planetary manager," someone specially equipped to define solutions to the planet's woes.[20] Continuing arid empire's tradition of privileging white male scientists as visionaries, the eco-catastrophism of the 1960s and '70s reinforced the Western scientist as a colonial hero (*in space!*) ready to save the day. And if the scientist-as-hero is the privileged voice warning of environmental collapse, he is also the one who is imagined to have the solutions. Both eco-catastrophism and its techno-optimist response thus bolster the "structures that privilege whiteness as the savior of our environmental future."[21]

If this new eco-aware Western scientist is to continue arid empire's pattern of neglecting the harm that he himself is inflicting on the natural environment and its non-white residents, he does so through a story that "we are all in this together." This is especially visible in the apocalyptic stories of interstellar exploration that gained strength in the '60s, and which continue to define contemporary expressions of eco-catastrophism. Today's techno-optimists, like the "billionaire space race" protagonists Elon Musk, Richard Branson, and Jeff Bezos, focus on Mars as a future home for humanity when Earth has succumbed to ecological collapse.[22] Like the imagery in *Dune*, the dramatic red rock landscape of Mars is frequently used as a powerful cue to alert people to the hardship of desert habitation.[23] To prepare for the eco-apocalypse and the trials of interplanetary living, then, it is not surprising that for decades visioneers of all stripes have treated the US Southwest as a testing ground.

As early as 1960, NASA started sending teams of astronauts to Nevada and Arizona for desert survival training.[24] There the astronauts dressed up in full space suits, pretending to be on the Moon at times, and at other times in mock Bedouin garb, headdress and all, pretending to be in the Arabian desert.[25] More recently, former NASA contractor and Mars Society president Robert Zubrin founded the Mars Desert Research Station in Utah. Funded by donations from SpaceX founder and Mars enthusiast Elon Musk, among others, the site was chosen for its desert landscape. As Zubrin explained to the *Los Angeles Times*, "We wanted a large theater of operations uninhabited, unvegetated and geologically interesting that we could explore."[26]

The newspaper's feature on the research station includes images of people romping around the Utah desert in space-suits, with red rock formations in the background, as if playing at being on Mars, just like the astronauts preparing to gambol across the Moon sixty years before. Regardless of whether today's romping about in spacesuits in the desert is best classified as genuine training or simply playing dress-up, the mediated spectacle of it all fuels a public image of Mars as a place to be colonized.[27] In this sense, projects like the Mars Desert Research Station normalize a colonial perspective of Mars, while also normalizing the colonial logic that prompted the settlement of the American Southwest in the first place. That is, if Utah is to represent Mars, Mars is also imagined to be Utah: the scampering white scientists are also playing colonizer.

Biosphere 2 was the brainchild of John P. Allen, an Oklahoma-born dilettante and eccentric with a bachelor's degree in metallurgy and a Harvard MBA. He became enchanted with the work of Buckminster Fuller, the American architect and futurist whose 1969 manifesto, *Operating Manual for Space-ship Earth*, launched him to fame. Allen was especially drawn to Fuller's Spaceship Earth concept, which was his techno-optimistic response to the crisis narratives of the late 1960s about Earth's resources being finite:

> In organizing our grand strategy we must first discover where we are now; that is, what our present navigational position in the universal scheme of evolution is. To begin our position—fixing aboard our Spaceship Earth we must first acknowledge that the abundance of immediately consumable, obviously desirable or utterly essential resources have been sufficient until now to allow us to carry on despite our ignorance. Being eventually exhaustible and spoilable, they have been adequate only up to this critical moment. This cushion-for-error of humanity's survival and growth up to now was apparently provided just as a bird inside of the egg is provided with liquid nutriment to develop it to a certain point. But then by design the nutriment is exhausted at just the time when the chick is large enough to be able to locomote on its own legs. And so as the chick pecks at the shell seeking more nutriment it inadvertently breaks open the shell. Stepping forth from its initial sanctuary, the young bird must now forage on its own legs and wings to discover the next phase of its regenerative sustenance.[28]

For Fuller, that "next phase" was rooted in human ingenuity and engineering prowess. John Allen determined to lead the search for new techno-fixes to "step forth" from earthly limits. "Western civilization isn't simply dying," he once said. "It's dead. We are probing into its ruins to take whatever is useful for the building of the new civilization to replace it."[29]

In the 1970s, Allen was leading a counterculture "ecovillage" commune in New Mexico, Synergia Ranch, where he met the wealthy Texas businessman Edward P. Bass.[30] The two shared an interest in environmental collapse, and in Bass, Allen found a receptive ear as he proposed to engineer artificial "biospheres" to prepare for the looming apocalypse and colonize

Mars. Bass ultimately contributed around $150 million to $200 million to the Biosphere 2 project, but in 1984, he pledged an initial $30 million and became chair of the company developing the project, Space Biospheres Ventures.[31] The project's leadership came from an exclusive crowd of Synergia acolytes, widely known to be members of the New Age cult that began at Allen's New Mexico commune.

With Bass's initial investment, the company secured land outside Tucson in 1984. Construction for Biosphere began in the mid-1980s, and the site's hyper-modern geodesic domes were specifically designed to evoke Bucky Fuller's Spaceship Earth concept. So eager was Space Biosphere Ventures to hitch their project to Fuller's vision that they hired one of the architect's former associates, Peter Jon Pearce, to design the facility and develop its special airtight sealing system.

Biosphere 2 was part of a longer trend in US higher education to position the Southwest as a region specializing in advanced scientific research related to space and astronomy. As early as 1894, when the Lowell Observatory was first opened in Flagstaff, Arizona, domed observatories quickly became icons for the region's new academic institutions to frame the Southwest as a kind of natural laboratory for high-tech observations: "Each new bulbous structure was a sign that science was on the rise in the region."[32] By 1922, the University of Arizona had opened the Steward Observatory on campus and, over decades, scientific leaders worked with political leaders and other boosters to advance the image of Arizona as a special place for space-related research.[33] This trend was amplified during the Cold War–era "space race," and Arizona was increasingly promoted as the home of cutting-edge research on all things space and solar—exemplified most vividly in a 1975 *Arizona Highways* magazine issue, "Solar Center, Arizona, U.S.A."

As this flashy image suggests, space aesthetics and future imaginaries started to permeate cultural life more generally,

**Figure 5.4.** *Front and back cover of a 1975* Arizona Highways *magazine special issue about solar power and space research in the desert.*

extending from research to design to science fiction. And it was precisely this vision of techno-futures in the Arizona desert that Biosphere 2 was drawing on and extending. It was yet another thread in arid empire's tapestry of envisioning the desert as a laboratory for high-tech, modern scientists. Here again, the desert backdrop works to bolster the settler story about the region's "natural" advantages for this industrial world-making and colonial world-taking. By infusing this established storyline with the spectacular space aesthetics that came to saturate popular culture during the Cold War, Biosphere 2 generated new excitement around bringing its visioneers' techno-futures to life in the Arizona desert.

The basic idea of the Biosphere 2 project was to develop a miniature world: "to create other microscale viable biospheric systems is to assist the Biosphere to evolve off planet Earth into potential life regions of our solar system."[34] According to Allen and his ally Mark Nelson, Biosphere 2 was supposed to be the first major step in preparing to colonize planets beyond

Earth. All they needed to do was create a mock-biosphere consisting of thousands of plants and animals, seven biomes, a complicated water- and gas-exchange system, and a crew of human-managers who would be the test crew. The Biospherians were supposed to subsist only on food they grew there and depend on gas and water exchanges engineered in advance. It was to be an entirely closed system, with two human experiments, one running from 1991–3, and the other for a ten-month period in 1994.

The closed system story was the crux of the whole project, and it was presented to the public as an amazing example of a self-sustaining ecology. But the Biospherians knew the project was not going to work: they had secret stores of food, stashed in advance. And it wasn't long before they had to tap those stores—but like the food itself, the act of consuming it was also kept secret. Besides food, other essentials like oxygen were in short supply. Even before the project started, the gas-exchange system didn't work. At one point in the first human experiment,

*Figure 5.5. A view from inside Bisophere 2.*

*Source:* Author, December 2019.

they had to admit to the public that oxygen was covertly being pumped in to keep the Biospherians alive. Nor were the highly mechanized water and energy systems self-sustaining. Far from being "completely" sealed off, the supposed Spaceship Earth prototype was in fact wholly dependent on Biosphere 1. Biosphere 2 residents, it turned out, were not much different from their predecessors romping in the desert playing dress-up for the spectacle of pseudo-science.

Serious scholars at UA largely felt that Biosphere 2 was hijacking the "good name" of science and the university. Many suspected that the project was not at all about benefiting humanity and advancing scientific frontiers, but rather a scheme through which the techno-optimists could make a profit. Serious researchers who participated in the project were asked to sign contracts giving Space Biosphere Ventures "worldwide, royalty-free irrevocable" rights to any "idea, concept, invention, patent or discovery" related to their work, creating further controversy in the established scientific community.[35] Beyond these unprecedented terms, the human "experiments" were critiqued because they were not based on accepted standards of experimental design. As one skeptical journalist said of Biosphere's fictive "scientific" recipe: "Take three or four thousand variables, enclose them in a glass container, throw in eight humans, shake 'em up like a margarita for two years, and in the end you'll get a nice, smooth blend."[36] The fact that the Biospherians were all members of the Synergia cult rather than neutral scientists added yet another layer to suspicions that the project had little to do with science.[37]

Even the entrepreneurial academics at UA who answered the call to help with various aspects of the project found working with Biosphere 2's visioneers to be a challenge. For example, Carl Hodges and members of the Environmental Research Laboratory were brought in to work on designing and setting up the plant biomes, based on their work with controlled environment agriculture. Researchers that I anonymously interviewed about the ERL were outraged by the non-scientific nature of the Biosphere project. Most pointed to it as a turning point in what had already been a downward slide for the laboratory and Hodges's shady financial dealings. No one could speak on the record about it (litigation was involved), but their message was clear: it was a sham and one of the most corrupt undertakings that they had witnessed.[38] Given that the ERL wasn't very clean even before this, this was a forceful message.

To this day, Biosphere 2's visioneers and acolytes insist it was "science, not a stunt."[39] But regardless of how one draws the boundaries around "science," Biosphere 2's visioneers were highly successful at mobilizing the apocalyptic narrative of environmental collapse to realize the project. And doing so allowed them to reap significant rewards. This included not just financial but also symbolic capital, as many used their newfound fame to promote themselves, their anxious visions of environmental collapse, and their popular press books.[40]

Mark Nelson's indefatigable defense of the project illustrates his own self-fashioning as a kind of environmental savior, similar to arid empire's other scientist-heroes, ready to teach the world how to survive in austere deserts, whether earthbound or not. Nelson later described his work as teaching humanity "a number of important lessons for improving our relationship with Earth's biosphere," a "relationship" that apparently included wholescale redesign. As he wrote, "we as a species have to learn how to become responsible participants of our biosphere, to come of age in our new Anthropocene."[41] Further: "The outmoded and false mythology of humans being uniquely 'above nature' is giving way to a new appreciation of our responsibility to our fellow species. On our beautiful and intricately connected 'Spaceship Earth,' we must make it work for everyone. Buckminster Fuller reminded us: 'It has to be everybody or nobody.'"[42]

Of course, "everybody" did not profit from the Biosphere 2 project. In laying claim to the Arizona land as a supposedly passive backdrop for their project, Space Biosphere Ventures re-entrenched the imperial history of treating the desert as a white man's "laboratory." The colonial logic that has always pervaded Biosphere 2 is perhaps best captured in a photograph that ran in the *Arizona Daily Star* in September 1991, marking the beginning of the first sealed human trial. The image is captioned: "Dan Old Elk, a Crow Indian from Montana, gives a blessing to the people of the Biosphere II program, during a brief ceremony before entering the facility which will be home for the next two years."[43]

Why a member of a tribe so far from the Sonoran desert was chosen for this ceremony is unclear. The symbolic effect is abundantly clear, however. The very act of enlisting such an individual, dressed in full traditional Indigenous garb and

*Source: Courtesy Arizona Daily Star, © 1991.*

**Figure 5.6.** *Photograph in the* Arizona Daily Star *in September 1991, when the Biospherians were beginning the first closed system experiment, with Crow leader Dan Old Elk giving a ceremonial "blessing."*

headdress, to "bless" the group of eight white men and women, dressed in their space-age jumpsuits, works to entrench colonial hierarchies of power, knowledge, visions of the future and past, science and tradition. Dan Old Elk here becomes not just an icon of tradition, but also an icon of arid empire: that a group of enlightened white settlers could harness the power of science to engineer solutions to overcome the desert's harsh limitations and, in so doing, "save" humanity.

Through its spectacle, Biosphere 2 affirmed the Anglo-American vision of the desert as a "natural" part of US territory —and that this was *good* because of the great scientific advances settlers were imagined to have brought to the land. The project's visioneers, with their claims to "solve" the planet's looming eco-apocalypse, echoed and reaffirmed the structures of white supremacy and control that their scientific predecessors had built through Arizona's scientific institutions. Biosphere 2's visioneers understood the power of science as spectacle—not only was the project given a progressive sheen through its connection with the University of Arizona, but also as packaged into a tourist attraction. When it first opened, thousands of visitors came each month and paid hefty entry fees. There were even initial discussions about developing a theme park around it.[44] That never materialized, and not long after, visitation dropped off precipitously.

Even before the spectacle began to wear off, the management of Space Biosphere Ventures under John Allen started to hemorrhage money, and the project became increasingly embroiled in controversy. This resulted in the project's expert advisory board quitting *en masse* in 1993. At this point, Biosphere 2's original sponsor Ed Bass brought in Steve Bannon (yes, *that* Steve Bannon—at this point working as an investment banker specializing in takeovers) to overhaul the company. Bannon removed Allen and his supporters in 1994 and arranged a deal with Columbia University to take over and run the project— which it did until it too became mired in controversy and its main advocate, Michael Crow, left to become the president of Arizona State University.[45]

Even the afterlife of Biosphere 2 shows how embroiled these projects are in both bad science and good PR, with a steady succession of businessmen finding new ways to trade on the fear of apocalypse and the promise of research dollars. After Columbia withdrew in 2003, the site went up for sale and was finally purchased by CDO Ranching & Development in 2007. That same year, the University of Arizona began leasing and operating the research facilities. With UA interests in the facility resurfacing at this transitional moment in 2007, the Bannon family also resurfaced: Steve Bannon's younger brother, Chris Bannon, was then installed as Biosphere 2's assistant director. He has largely kept a low profile at the university but appears to have primarily concentrated on Biosphere 2 fundraising efforts, reflected in his subsequent move to the UA Development Office, where he still works and is handsomely remunerated today.[46]

In 2011, UA resumed complete control of Biosphere 2 after CDO decided to donate the facilities and forty acres of the site's land to the university. Ed Bass also helped with the transition, giving a fresh $20 million grant through his Philecology Foundation, and lauding UA's "passionate commitment to Biosphere 2 and its capacity to explore the urgent questions relating to the sustainability of our planet Earth."[47] In 2017, Bass followed this up with yet another grant, this one for $30 million. UA leaders reciprocated Bass's earlier praise, with the Biosphere 2 director, Joaquin Ruiz, declaring, "The world needs people like Mr. Ed Bass, with his unique vision and passion to make a positive impact on our world."[48] Bass's attention-grabbing donation displays notwithstanding, Biosphere is still shrouded in secrecy, and no archival records are open to the public. University administrators are always keen to maintain the goodwill of a generous donor, and for this reason it is unsurprising that the University of Arizona continues to maintain the positive spin of Biosphere 2 being a place of "science, not a stunt."[49]

Biosphere nonetheless operates today without the same imaginative pull of spectacle as before. This is not for want of trying: its supporters continue to justify it using the same tropes of environmental apocalypse and dreams of colonizing Mars. For instance, one of the newest Biosphere 2 projects is SAM (Space Analog for the Moon and Mars), which is described as a "hi-fidelity, hermetically sealed habitat analog" for teams seeking to spend a few days or months living in sealed-off extraterrestrial conditions. The vision of tech entrepreneur Kai Staats, SAM is supposed to be returning to "the origin of the iconic Biosphere 2 and a look to the future as we prepare to become an interplanetary species."[50] In the figure of Staats and others involved in this project, we see that Biosphere 2 also still features the same colonial scientist-as-hero figures as before, now revamping and repackaging the facility's promise to use the "natural" advantages of the desert to inspire new ways to geo-engineer our way out of climate catastrophe.

In Biosphere 2's techno-fetishistic future-oriented focus, looking to the past is generally discouraged. Nonetheless, on the fringes of the facility's modern domes, Biosphere today hosts an impressive display about Omani *aflaj* channels—traditional water systems for supporting agriculture in the Arabian desert. The display itself seems like a remnant of older versions of arid empire, and indeed, the story of its construction illustrates how connections between Arizona and Arabia are continually revived and reimagined. The man behind the *aflaj* display was an Omani UA alumnus who had a longstanding interest in Biosphere 2, but the idea for the exhibit was hatched only after the University of Arizona helped organize an exhibition on the Phoenix Mars mission in Oman.

Sultan bin Hamdoon Al Harthi, the former mayor of Muscat, received his bachelor's and master's degrees from the

University of Arizona's architecture program.[51] During his time at the university, he befriended Peter Smith, who had worked with the UA Lunar and Planetary Laboratory since 1978.[52] Smith developed the camera used on NASA's 1997 Mars Pathfinder mission and several subsequent Mars missions, and then served as a principal investigator in the Phoenix Mars Lander mission that reached the red planet in 2008 to "study the history of water in the Martian arctic" and "search for evidence of a habitable zone."[53]

Al Harthi took great interest in this work and invited Smith to host an exhibit about the Phoenix mission in Oman. During Smith's visit to Oman, the two men started talking about the cosmos, and Al Harthi reflected on the long Omani tradition of looking to the stars for water management, a practice tied to its ancient *falaj* system. Out of this conversation came the idea that this Omani tradition should be given similar attention in the United States as was given to Smith's Mars exhibit in Oman. Smith suggested that Biosphere 2 would be a suitable place for a permanent exhibit because it would receive regular visits from tourists and scientists alike. Al Harthi then got connected with Biosphere 2 staff to realize the project.

The UA Development office took interest in the potential alumni support that might be reaped from such a project, but Al Harthi actually used his personal connections at the Omani Sultan Qaboos Cultural Center to secure a $298,000 grant for the display, framed as a model *falaj* called "Water Oasis."[54] The exhibit was opened to great fanfare in 2012, but after the grant money was received, the project was quickly relegated to oblivion. Today, tours do not take visitors there, the water has been turned off, and the site itself is rapidly decaying. The desert story, like the desert itself, can be profitable when it is cultivated. Such opportunities for profit can be intermittent, and when the revenue ceases, the spectacle does too.

Today, guides are instructed not to take visitors to the display. Instead, they are shuttled to the exhibits inside the

Source: Author, December 2019.

*Figure 5.7. Outdoor display on Omani culture and* aflaj *system at Biosphere 2.*

main complex, which feature the hypermodern visuals that were wholly absent from the tradition-oriented display about Omani water conservation techniques practiced for thousands of years. A recent display about "Farming on Mars," for example, showcased UA researchers' NASA-funded work at Biosphere 2 toward future agriculture on the red planet. Placards enthusiastically told visitors (presumably children) that farmers and Mars explorers are wanted … outfitted in spacesuits, of course. Old ideas die hard in this arid empire. Or rather, they don't die: they just get reinvented, repackaged, and repurposed.

Techno-fetishistic dreams for extraterrestrial futures bring together both the science and the fiction in this iteration of arid empire. As mentioned already, the passion for colonizing Mars and Outer Space has attracted huge investments from today's Silicon Valley tech entrepreneurs Musk, Branson, and

**Figure 5.8.** *Placards on display in the Biosphere 2 exhibit on current research for a "Farming on Mars" project.*

**Figure 5.9.** *Display in the Biosphere 2 "Farming on Mars" exhibit on "Lunar Greenhouse Habitat modules."*

Bezos. The effort of UA's current leadership at Biosphere 2 to link it up with the university's established planetary science institutions—and to expand them through large new NASA grants and other space programs—reflects the broader funding environment that continues to encourage this kind of research across the United States.

This Mars enthusiasm isn't limited to the US; it has been all the rage in the UAE too. The country established a space agency in 2014 in Abu Dhabi, when its emir and UAE president Sheikh Khalifa bin Zayed Al Nahyan also announced the Emirates Mars Mission. That mission resulted in the 2020 launching of the Mars orbiter "Hope," which in turn enabled the UAE in 2021 to proudly boast of becoming the first Arab country to reach that planet.[55] Developing a space industry was formally identified as a "primary national objective" in 2015. Later space schemes include one with the stated aim of enabling the UAE to establish "the first inhabitable human settlement on Mars by 2117."[56]

The Emirati push to advance its Mars programs might appear to be an effort to join the US tech billionaires' space race, but it is more fundamentally about the leadership's effort to define the UAE's "post-oil" development trajectory around a high-tech, science-based knowledge economy. An earlier example of this development agenda was the Masdar eco-city project, which took inspiration from Arcosanti and Biosphere 2 as exemplary sites to demo techno-modern futures in the face of environmental apocalypse. Like the projects before it, the Masdar project understood that the desert setting was essential to underwriting the visioneers' claims that their ostensible goals—to save humanity and prepare for life on Mars—were certainly not about venality.

The United Arab Emirates started construction in 2006 on a new "carbon-neutral" eco-city, called Masdar City, to model an urban form that can confront the challenges of climate change through high-tech design and sustainability R&D. The project is generously financed by the Emirati sovereign wealth fund and designed by the influential British architectural firm Foster + Partners. The research element of the project, the Masdar Institute of Science and Technology, was developed in partnership with the Massachusetts Institute of Technology and became the anchor tenant in 2010. But the science underway at the Masdar Institute was always secondary to the visual spectacle of the eco-city project, broadcast through its architecture.

Masdar City was supposed to become a gleaming exemplar of sustainable urban design in the austere hinterlands of Abu Dhabi.[57] Though the Institute was actually built, the broader eco-city plan for a community of 50,000 people was never realized and has since been written off as a failure.[58] Masdar was nonetheless effective at grabbing ample media attention for the UAE's story about promoting environmental sustainability. The spectacle of the project was enhanced by being visually and rhetorically positioned as an eco-friendly "oasis" in the Arabian desert—a living laboratory for alternative futures in the face of environmental catastrophe.

Masdar's lead designer, Norman Foster, was also enchanted with outer space and, like Biosphere's John Allen, infatuated with Buckminster Fuller's Spaceship Earth concept. Foster met Fuller in 1971, actively studied his work, and has since continued to expand on the longer genealogy of outer space designs that became increasingly popular in the 1970s. As one Foster + Partners architect working on the project explained, "Norman wants to be the Bucky Fuller of this century."[59] Extraterrestrial desolation continued to be on Foster's mind as he worked on the Masdar project, which he even framed as a "spaceship in the desert" and compared the practice of architecture in the Arabian Peninsula to lunar exploration: "The inhospitable terrain suggests that the only way to survive here is with the maximum of technological support, a bit like living on the moon."[60] The Emirati desert might appear "a bit like living

**Figure 5.10.** *View of a futuristic spaceship–style building at Masdar.*

on the moon" to this white British starchitect, but it is not the Moon. Just as the U.S. Southwest is not Mars.

Foster certainly couldn't visit the Moon for his research, but he did travel to Arizona to visit Arcosanti in preparing for the Masdar commission. Beyond their architectural design, sites like Arcosanti or the Fuller-inspired Biosphere 2 demonstrated how techno-optimistic "living labs" could generate significant money and prestige even as they repackaged and repurposed the established storyline of eco-catastrophism. This capitalist storytelling is an art that Norman Foster understood well. One of the most prominent architects in recent history, he found quick success in transforming himself into a globally sought-after brand. Foster exhibits few qualms about accepting commissions and attaching his name to the projects, while letting his staff assume responsibility for nearly all the work.[61] In paying Foster's hefty fees, the UAE's state-owned Mubadala Development Company was buying a brand to attach to Masdar. Foster may be a more mainstream figure than the other visioneers we have seen at work in this chapter, but his vision for Masdar was similar to Biosphere 2 in that it captured the dystopian vision of environmental apocalypse to sell just another ill-conceived desert experiment as a utopia for humanity's future on Mars.

These diverse outer-space references might seem innocuous at first blush. They admit to being a "model" or "exemplar"— just for show, just for practice. They admit their theatrics. And yet, they are real things in the world, for which real people make real money. The spectacle may be fake, but it has real consequences for how power and prestige get allocated. The people selling these test projects might know their experiments will never be scaled up, that nobody will seek to replicate their pilot project. Some might do so unwittingly, or they may naively believe in their own sales pitch. Regardless, they can reap huge rewards all the same, whether those include the material benefits of securing grant money or other financial rewards, advancing one's scientific career, gaining access to a platform to broadcast an ideological or political agenda, securing personal or institutional prestige, assuaging settler colonial guilt, or denying it entirely. Whatever the rewards may be, the experiment becomes an end in itself.[62]

So even if an experiment never serves as a model—Biosphere 2 never was a closed system and it never illustrated how humanity could "evolve off" planet Earth, just as the UAE's Mars 2117 project will probably never result in a habitable Mars colony—the prototype is effective because it uses *realism* to suggest that the idea is *realistic*. The model allows observers to "see (or at least imagine)" that the techno-futures on display could actually be realized, even if they are theatrical.[63] The spectacle of the prototype is indifferent to the "reality" of the vision on display; rather, it is designed to amplify the message or critique that it advances. In short, spectacle is just the tool for selling the product as something more than science fiction.

By the 1970s, visioneers in Arizona had learned to use science *and* fiction to advance their interests and to sell their impressive new schemes for the future. And for them, arid empire was no longer terrestrially bound to Earth: it included other desert planets too. It should be no surprise, then, that their Emirati successors joyfully celebrated the UAE's Mars Mission entering orbit in February 2021. "Hope," the probe's name, neatly encapsulates the spirit of techno-optimism that has radiated out from apocalyptic visions of environmental collapse since the 1960s and continues in today's anxiety about climate change. In the apocalyptic stories that underpin Arcosanti, Biosphere 2, and Masdar, the white settler is never the culprit but the savior, preparing to engineer a solution to the imagined future ecological collapse. In this iteration of arid empire, its visioneers continue to silence the "already existing dystopias" of Indigenous colonization.[64] To see double, as in Cressey's Camel/Coke visual, is to recognize that from this perspective, arid empire already is, and always has been, apocalyptic.

# 6

## Deserts

*In which we learn to see the political lives of deserts.*

In the Western imagination, deserts are places of desolation, emptiness, social and environmental extremes, or just wastelands. But they are also romanticized, as in the pastoral tradition. In a 1937 article introducing the first issue of *Desert Magazine*, the founders, writing from El Centro, California, present these divergent narrative traditions and decry the narrow, negative depiction of arid lands: "[T]he stranger and the uninitiated see only the mask. The other Desert—the real Desert—is not for the eyes of the superficial observer, or the fearful soul or the cynic. It is a land, the character of which is hidden except to those who come with friendliness and understanding."[1] The "real Desert," they assert, is a place of beauty and inspiration. As someone who grew up in Arizona's Sonoran Desert, I tend to agree.

But as I noted in opening this book, my home is also a place of violence. In practice and in popular culture, the Arizona desert has served as the stage for imperial dramas of frontier masculinity, genocide, and the modernist violence of subverting Nature to the will of Man. Even before US colonization, the land now called Arizona was eyed for projects of extraction under the Spanish empire. The coming of American empire was a turning point, as the extractive agenda of the growing country commodified its diverse resources—flora, fauna, sand, water, minerals—in service of building its economy, its territorial reach, and its global influence. To take control of this land, though, the US state needed more than the military: it also needed farmers and scientists like those from the University of Arizona, looking to the Middle East to make the desert "bloom."

The history of Arizona and Arabia's entangled fates may at first appear exceptional. But their entanglement represents a much broader history of arid empire that was impossible without the global connections brought to life by the scientists and experts who mastered the narrative and material resources of the desert. So even if the Western tradition is full of tropes about deserts as wastelands, it also encompasses a rich tradition of transforming the desert into a place with great significance and political potential. The lustful fantasies of dominance, wealth, and territorial control that bind Arizona and Arabia may have escaped our attention for decades, but by *seeing* the connections of these two deserts, invisibility itself comes into focus as the crux of arid empire's uncanny power. In recovering some of these connections—of dates, diplomacy, desal, and dreams—I have tried to understand why they keep getting reinvented. Every decade, scientific "innovations" build on the same tropes and ideas of the desert as a blank slate to enact some grand vision rather than being someone else's home.

Americans don't often like to think about their country's imperial past, let alone its imperial present.[2] Or, at least, we are not usually trained to carefully reflect on it. For me, then, in looking at Cressey's Camel/Coke double exposure, and realizing my blindness to the multiple layers of arid empire that made such an image possible (and made my own discovery of it possible), I was forced to reckon with my role as a descendant of empire. At the beginning of this book, I observed that my childhood romance with the desert was a political *achievement*: it was the result of the calculated effort of countless white settlers who envisioned someone like me living out their vision of civilization in the desert Southwest. I was not conscious of this as a child, but I was nonetheless complicit in enacting this arid empire through the simplest place-making practice of all: calling Arizona home.

When I later became a geographer and a scholar of the Arabian Peninsula, I reveled in the region's desert landscapes because they reminded me of home. But for many years, I wasn't paying attention to how my Arizona upbringing, as a descendent of America's arid empire, bound me to the region in other ways. Thinking with Cressey's Camel/Coke image as a way to see double, to see across time, to see across space, I have come to understand that I am just one traveler in a long succession of others who traveled to Arabia from Arizona. Some of the American travelers before me went there self-consciously working in the service of building US empire and, other times, they went in service of ideals structured by the language of science and arid lands research. These men (and some women) have thus extracted identities from deserts: building careers and entire academic institutions around expertise in drylands, arid lands, and various claims to a special knowledge of the desert. But in all cases, including my own, they were building from the original arid empire built in the American West.

When I first started looking at the exchanges between Arizona and the Arabian Peninsula, I was baffled by their sheer persistence over the decades. How is it, I found myself asking, that these ties keep getting reinvented and renewed across nearly 150 years? The answer is that deserts lead curiously political lives. Whereas I first interpreted their interconnections as chance, I have sought to show in this book that they are more than that: they represent a geopolitical structure that binds the United States and the Middle East. And yet they are also embodied by specific people, each of whom finds their own way to navigate this structure. For the ties between Arizona and Arabia to stick, they had to be brought to life by real people. The story of arid empire illustrates how the "desert" is both a place and a story that has significant political strength. Agents of arid empire are those who found creative ways to breathe life into the story of the "desert" as a place of cooperation and mutual understanding, and to put this story to work in the name of science, the state, and all range of other agendas.

The political lives of deserts are ultimately about who gets to define and control the story of what the "real Desert" is. The people who try to control this story have their own agendas and aspirations, but more often than not, they ignore the significance of the desert's materiality. That is, they ignore the fact that the landscapes and resources and physical geography of the Sonoran and Arabian deserts are vastly different. They ignore the violence of tapping their water reserves unsustainably, or casting them as blank slate "laboratories" for techno-science. They ignore the significance of other ways of knowing and existing within arid environments. They ignore the harms of imperialism's extractive impulse.

Arid empire is a structure of power made possible by its very invisibility—but if we choose to see it, perhaps we can refuse its violence and give the possibility of life back to the desert. In reflecting on the tragic loss of migrant lives in Arizona's borderlands in recent years, Tohono O'odham poet Ofelia Zepeda reminds us in her poem "Not the Intent of This Desert":

> Every tiny blade of creosote leaf has a memory of the people
>     that have come through.
> The sand absorbs the tears, nightmares, sorrows of the
>     walkers.
> It muffles their cries.
> No one can hear them.
> This was never the intent of this desert.[3]

Tohono O'odham means "desert people," so for her community, the desert is home. It need not be a cruel, militarized landscape. It is life and it is possibility. And for someone like me to have the privilege to be born on Tohono O'odham lands and to listen to Dr. Zepeda recite this poem at the end of my journey through arid empire's history, I hear her enjoinder not to give the desert over to the violence. For me too, it is home, life, and possibility.

# Notes

## 1. Double Exposure

1  Fred S. Perrine, "Uncle Sam's Camel Corps." *New Mexico Historical Review* 1, no. 1 (1926), 436. See also Walter L. Fleming, "Jefferson Davis's Camel Experiment." *Popular Science* 74 (February 1909); Chris Heller, "Whatever Happened to the Wild Camels of the American West?" *Smithsonian Magazine* (August 6, 2015), smithsonian.com; Andrew C. Isenberg, "'A Land of Hardship and Distress': Camels, North American Deserts and the Limits of Conquest." *Global Environment* 12, no. 1 (2019), 84–101; Gary Paul Nabhan, "Camel Whisperers: Desert Nomads Crossing Paths." *The Journal of Arizona History* 49, no. 2 (2008), 95–118; J.W. Palmer, "The Ship of the Desert." *Harper's New Monthly Magazine* 15, no. 89 (1857), 578–93; John Shapard, "The United States Army Camel Corps: 1856–66." *Military Review* LV, no. 8 (August 1975), 77–89.
2  Benedict R. Anderson, *Imagined Communities: Reflections on the Origin and Spread of Nationalism* (London: Verso, 1983).
3  Paul Frymer, *Building an American Empire: The Era of Territorial and Political Expansion* (Princeton: Princeton University Press, 2017); Patricia Nelson Limerick, *The Legacy of Conquest: The Unbroken Past of the American West* (New York: Norton, 1987).
4  Walter L. Hixson, *American Settler Colonialism: A History* (New York: Palgrave Macmillan, 2013); Janne Lahti, *Cultural Construction of Empire: The U.S. Army in Arizona and New Mexico* (Lincoln: University of Nebraska Press, 2012); Dennis Reinhartz and Gerald Saxon, *Mapping and Empire: Soldier-Engineers on the Southwestern Frontier* (Austin: University of Texas Press, 2005).
5  Arthur A. Gray, Francis P. Farquhar, and William S. Lewis, *Camels in Western America* (San Francisco: California Historical Society, 1930), 3–4.

6 George P. Marsh, "Lecture on the Camel: Delivered Before the Smithsonian Institution." Smithsonian Institution (1854), 4. See also George P. Marsh, *The Camel: His Organization, Habits, and Uses* (Boston: Gould and Lincoln, 1856).

7 Marsh, "Lecture," 20.

8 Ibid., 23–4.

9 Richard Slotkin, *Gunfighter Nation: The Myth of the Frontier in Twentieth-Century America* (New York: Maxwell Macmillan, 1992); Henry Nash Smith, *Virgin Land: The American West as Symbol and Myth* (Cambridge: Harvard University Press, 1950).

10 Andrew Curley, "*Resources* Is Just Another Word for Colonialism." In *The Routledge Handbook of Critical Resource Geography*, edited by Matthew Himley, Elizabeth Havice, and Gabriela Valdivia (New York: Routledge, 2021), 79–89.

11 Ned Blackhawk, *Violence Over the Land: Indians and Empires in the Early American West* (Cambridge: Harvard University Press, 2006); Roxanne Dunbar-Ortiz, *An Indigenous Peoples' History of the United States* (Boston: Beacon Press, 2014); Ward Churchill, *Struggle for the Land: Indigenous Resistance to Genocide, Ecocide, and Expropriation in Contemporary North America* (Monroe: Common Courage Press, 1993); Joe Lockard, "Carceral Colonialism in Arizona Territory." *Western American Literature* 55, no. 1 (2020), 1–31; Richard Slotkin, *Regeneration Through Violence: The Mythology of the American Frontier, 1600–1860* (Middletown: Wesleyan University Press, 1973); Patrick Wolfe, "Settler Colonialism and the Elimination of the Native." *Journal of Genocide Research* 8, no. 4 (2006), 387–409.

12 Diana K. Davis, *The Arid Lands: History, Power, Knowledge* (Cambridge: MIT Press, 2016); Diana K. Davis, "From the Divine to the Desertified: The Foundational Case of Deserts in the Middle East." *Global Environment* 12, no. 1 (2019), 56–83; Richard V. Francaviglia, *Go East, Young Man: Imagining the American West as the Orient* (Logan: Utah State University Press, 2011).

13 Catrin Gersdorf, *The Poetics and Politics of the Desert: Landscape and the Construction of America* (Amsterdam: Brill Rodopi, 2009), 129.

14 Stephen Bonsal, *Edward Fitzgerald Beale* (New York: G. P. Putnam's Sons, 1912); Harlan Davey Fowler, *Camels to California* (Stanford: Stanford University Press, 1950); Lewis Burt Lesley, *Uncle Sam's Camels: The Journal of May Humphreys Stacey Supplemented by the Report of Edward Fitzgerald Beale (1857–1858)* (Cambridge: Harvard University Press, 1929); Gerald Thompson, *Edward F. Beale & the American West* (Albuquerque: University of New Mexico Press, 1983).

15 *San Francisco Evening Bulletin* (January 25, 1858), 3 (quoted in Bonsal, *Edward Fitzgerald Beale*, 205).

16 Bonsal, *Edward Fitzgerald Beale;* Lesley, *Uncle Sam's Camels;* Perrine, "Uncle Sam's Camel Corps"; Shapard, "The United States"; Thompson, *Edward F. Beale.*

17 Slotkin, *Gunfighter Nation.*

18 Nick Estes, speaking on "Red Power Hour Ep. 5: Fighting Settler Fascism w/ Justine & Brandon," *The Red Nation Podcast,* therednation.org. See also Vine Deloria Jr., *Custer Died for Your Sins: An Indian Manifesto* (Norman: University of Oklahoma Press, 1988).

19 Philip G. Jones and Anna Kenny, *Australia's Muslim Cameleers: Pioneers of the Inland, 1860s–1930s* (Kent Town: Wakefield Press, 2010).

## 2. Dates

1 Susan McGinley, "UA-Led $3.9M Project to Focus on Date Palm Production in Oman." *UA News* (2019), news.arizona.edu.

2 Diwan of Royal Court, "About Us." *Million Date Palm Plantation Project* (2020), mdp.gov.om/about

3 Quoted in McGinley, "UA-Led $3.9M Project."

4 Roger L. Geiger, *The History of American Higher Education: Learning and Culture From the Founding to World War II* (Princeton: Princeton University Press, 2015); Roger L. Geiger and Nathan M. Sorber, *The Land-Grant Colleges and the Reshaping of American Higher Education* (London: Transaction, 2013); Robert Lee and Tristan Ahtone, "Land-Grab Universities: Expropriated Indigenous Land Is the Foundation of the Land-Grant University System." *High Country News* 52, no. 4 (March 30, 2020); Nathan M. Sorber, *Land-Grant Colleges and Popular Revolt: The Origins of the Morrill Act and the Reform of Higher Education* (Ithaca: Cornell University Press, 2018).

5 Geiger, *The History,* 304–6.

6 Frymer, *Building an American Empire,* 23–5.

7 Lee and Ahtone, "Land-Grab Universities."

8 Margaret Mitchell, "The Founding of the University of Arizona 1885–1894." *Arizona and the West* 27, no. 1 (1985), 5–36; Virginia E. Rice, "The Arizona Agricultural Experiment Station: A History to 1917." *Arizona and the West* 20, no. 2 (1978), 123–40.

9 Frank A. Gulley, *Arizona Agricultural Experiment Station Bulletin* 1 (1890).

10 Ibid.

11  Frieda Knobloch, *The Culture of Wilderness: Agriculture as Colonization in the American West* (Chapel Hill: University of North Carolina Press, 1996); Margaret Walsh, *The American West: Visions and Revisions* (New York: Cambridge University Press, 2005).

12  Letter to Hon. Edw. Willits, As. Sec., Agricultural Dept., Washington, DC, July 18th, 1891. University of Arizona Special Collections, AZ 406, Box 1, 1891 Letterbook, F.A. Gulley, 1–2.

13  David W. Adams, *Education for Extinction: American Indians and the Boarding School Experience, 1875–1928* (Lawrence: University Press of Kansas, 1995). On the contemporary situation, see Emma Ascott, "Enduring Trauma: Arizona's Indigenous Boarding Schools Will Be Investigated, Interior Announces." *Tucson Weekly* (July 1, 2021).

14  Letter to Hon. Edw. Willits, As. Sec., Agricultural Dept., Washington, DC, July 18th, 1891. University of Arizona Special Collections, AZ 406, Box 1, 1891 Letterbook, F.A. Gulley, 2.

15  Richard A. Harvill, "Forward." In *The Lamp in the Desert: The Story of the University of Arizona*, Douglas D. Martin. (Tucson: University of Arizona Press, 1960), vi.

16  Emma Gibson, "Racial Bias and Indigenous Communities on Arizona Campuses." *Arizona Spotlight, Arizona Public Media* (February 26, 2020).

17  Frymer, *Building an American Empire*, 23. See also Katherine Benton-Cohen, *Borderline Americans: Racial Division and Labor War in the Arizona Borderlands* (Cambridge: Harvard University Press, 2009); Eric Meeks, *Border Citizens: The Making of Indians, Mexicans, and Anglos in Arizona* (Austin: University of Texas Press, 2007).

18  Quoted in Frymer, *Building an American Empire*, 198.

19  Frymer, *Building an American Empire*, 198.

20  Frymer, *Building an American Empire*, 175–6, 204; Meeks, *Border Citizens*, 36–43; Benton-Cohen, *Borderline Americans*, 172–3.

21  Benton-Cohen, *Borderline Americans*, 186.

22  William E. Smythe, *The Conquest of Arid America* (New York: Harper & Brothers, 1900), xvi.

23  Majed Akhter and Kerri Jean Ormerod, "The Irrigation Technozone: State Power, Expertise, and Agrarian Development in the U.S. West and British Punjab, 1880–1920." *Geoforum* 60 (2015), 123–32; Andrew Curley, "Infrastructures as Colonial Beachheads: The Central Arizona Project and the Taking of Navajo Resources." *Environment and Planning D: Society and Space* 39, no. 3 (2021), 387–404; Andrew Curley, "'Our Winters' Rights': Challenging Colonial Water Laws." *Global Environmental Politics* 19, no. 3

(2019), 57–76; Andrew Curley, "Unsettling Indian Water Settlements: The Little Colorado River, the San Juan River, and Colonial Enclosures." *Antipode* 53, no. 3 (2021), 705–23; Donald Worster, *Rivers of Empire: Water, Aridity, and the Growth of the American West* (New York: Pantheon, 1985).

24 John H. Cady, *Arizona's Yesterday: Being the Narrative of John H. Cady, Pioneer (Rewritten and Revised by Basil Dillon Woon)* (Los Angeles: Times-Minor Printing and Binding House, 1916), 27.

25 Benton-Cohen, *Borderline Americans*, 173.

26 Benton-Cohen, *Borderline Americans*, 186.

27 Katherine Heslop, "Making the Desert Blossom: Spreading the Gospel of Irrigation." *Journal of the Southwest* 56, no. 1 (2014), 29–51.

28 Meeks, *Border Citizens*, 33–5. See also Dunbar-Ortiz, *An Indigenous Peoples' History*; Philip VanderMeer, *Desert Visions and the Making of Phoenix, 1860–2009* (Albuquerque: University of New Mexico Press, 2010).

29 Silvester Mowry, *The Geography and Resources of Arizona and Sonora: An Address Before the American Geographical and Statistical Society* (New York: A. Roman & Co, 1863), 16. UAIR History of Agriculture & Rural Life digital archive.

30 Schultz & Franklin Immigration Solicitors, *Salt River Valley, South Side: The Fruit Belt of Arizona* (Tempe, 1892). UAIR History of Agriculture & Rural Life digital archive.

31 "Addenda: Extract from letter of N. R. Gibson, Esq., of Peoria, dated June 10th, 1885, in reply to inquiries from S. A. Kean & Co., of Chicago." *The Garden of America: The Salt River Valley, Maricopa County, Arizona* (1885), 19. UAIR History of Agriculture & Rural Life digital archive.

32 Patrick Hamilton, *Salt River Valley: Its Attractions for the Capitalist, the Invalid, the Immigrant* (Phoenix: Phoenix and Maricopa County board of Trade, 1800s), 2. UAIR History of Agriculture & Rural Life digital archive.

33 Ibid., 11.

34 "Arizona, Salt River Valley," brochure issued by the Santa Fe Railway Company (1909), 3. UAIR History of Agriculture & Rural Life digital archive.

35 Charles Colley, "Arizona, Cradle of the American Date Growing Industry, 1890–1916." *Southern California Quarterly* 53, no. 1 (1971), 55.

36 Matthew S. Hopper, "Globalization and the Economics of African Slavery in Arabia in the Age of Empire." *Journal of African Development* 12, no. 1 (2010), 163.

37 Matthew S. Hopper, *Slaves of One Master: Globalization and*

*Slavery in Arabia in the Age of Empire* (New Haven: Yale University Press, 2015), 54.

38 Hopper, "Globalization," 164.

39 Colley, "Arizona, Cradle," 55; Charles Colley, "The Desert Shall Blossom: North African Influence on the American Southwest." *The Western Historical Quarterly* 14, no. 3 (1983), 277–90; Richard Haney, *The University of Arizona College of Agriculture: A Century of Discovery!* (Tucson: University of Arizona Press, 1985); Glenn C. Wright, "The Commercial Date Industry in the United States and Mexico." *HortScience* 51, no. 11 (2016), 1333–8.

40 D. Rivera, D. Johnson, J. Delgadillo, M. H. Carrillo, C. Obón, R. Krueger, F. Alcaraz, S. Ríos, and E. Carreño, "Historical Evidence of the Spanish Introduction of Date Palm (*Phoenix Dactylifera L., Arecaceae*) into the Americas." *Genetic Resources and Crop Evolution* 60, no. 4 (2013), 1433–52; Mary Lawson Neef, "Date Culture in the Southwest." *Out West* 27, no. 2 (August 1907), 115–25; Paul Popenoe, *Date Growing in the Old World and the New* (Los Angeles: George Rice & Sons, 1913).

41 Colley, "Arizona, Cradle," 55–6.

42 Donald Hodel and Dennis Johnson, *Imported and American Varieties of Dates (Phoenix Dactylifera) in the United States* (Oakland: University of California Agriculture and Natural Resources, 2007), 3.

43 Sterling Evans, *Farming Across Borders: A Transnational History of the North American West* (College Station: Texas A&M University Press, 2017); Jared Farmer, *Trees in Paradise: A California History* (New York: W.W. Norton & Company, 2013); Katherine G. Morrissey and Marcus A. Burtner, "Global Imaginary of Arid Lands: Early Twentieth-Century United States Botanists in Africa." *Global Environment* 12, no. 1 (2019), 102–33; John B. Seitz, "Imagining Alfalfastan: Plant Exploration, Technopolitics, Colonialism, and the Environment in the American West and Russian Central Asia, 1897–1930." *Agricultural History* 95, no. 3 (2021), 444–71; Omar Tesdell, "Territoriality and the Technics of Drylands Science in Palestine and North America." *International Journal of Middle East Studies* 47, no. 3 (2015), 570–3.

44 Letter from Jared G. Smith, Washington, DC, December 14, 1900. University of Arizona Special Collections, AZ 446, Box 14, Folder 2.

45 David Fairchild, *Persian Gulf Dates and Their Introduction Into America* (Washington: US Department of Agriculture, 1903); David Fairchild, *The World Was My Garden: Travels of a Plant*

*Explorer* (London: C. Scribner's Sons, 1938); Daniel Stone, *The Food Explorer: The True Adventures of the Globe-Trotting Botanist Who Transformed What America Eats* (New York: Dutton, 2018); Walter T. Swingle, *The Date Palm and Its Utilization in the Southwestern States* (Washington: US Department of Agriculture, 1904).

46  James W. Toumey, "The Date Palm." *Arizona Agricultural Experiment Station Bulletin* 29 (1898), 114.

47  Ibid., 148.

48  Charles Colley, *The Century of Robert H. Forbes: The Career of a Pioneer Agriculturist, Agronomist, Environmentalist, Conservationist, and Water Specialist in Arizona and Abroad* (Tucson: Arizona Historical Society, 1977).

49  Scott Trafton, *Egypt Land: Race and Nineteenth-Century American Egyptomania* (Durham: Duke University Press, 2004).

50  Colley, "The Desert Shall," 281.

51  Robert Forbes, "Date Palm Culture—A Word in Time." *Agricultural Experiment Station Bulletin* 24 (1900), 107–9.

52  Knobloch, *The Culture of Wilderness*, 1.

53  "A Plan to Utilize a Desert." *Scientific American* 38 (1878), 175.

54  "Date Palms for Arizona." *Scientific American* 80 (1899), 284.

55  "The Deglet Noor the Date for Arizona." *Arizona Republic* (December 21, 1910), 2.

56  Monroe Woolley, Growing our own dates. Scientific American, 115, no. 11 (1916), 244–244.

57  T. J. Gridley. Foreword: Report of the First Date Grower's Institute at Coachella (1924). University of Arizona Institutional Repository, uair.library.arizona.edu/item/294084

58  Hodel and Johnson, *Imported and American Varieties of Dates*, p. 6; Mary A. McCarthy, "Date Palms in the Desert: Reimagining and Cooperating with Nature in Arid Arizona." Arizona Journal of Interdisciplinary Studies 1 (2012): 39–53.

59  "The Final Success of Date Culture." *Arizona Republic* (December 21, 1910), 2.

60  The demise of Gulf date economies is actually part of a much broader story, which should not be whitewashed: the viability of this sector in Oman depended largely on slavery, which was not outlawed in that country until 1970. See Hopper, "Globalization"; Hopper, *Slaves of One Master.*

61  Michael E. Latham, *The Right Kind of Revolution: Modernization, Development, and U.S. Foreign Policy From the Cold War to the Present* (Ithaca: Cornell University Press, 2011).

62  Wright, "The Commercial Date Industry," 1337.

## 3. Diplomacy

1 "Saudi Hay Farm in Arizona Tests State's Supply of Groundwater." National Public Radio (November 2, 2015).

2 "Water Issues/Saudi-Arabian Farming in Arizona." Arizona PBS, YouTube (September 30, 2016).

3 Nathan Halverson, "What California Can Learn From Saudi Arabia's Water Mystery." *Reveal News* (April 22, 2015); "Saudi Land Purchases in California and Arizona Fuel Debate Over Water Rights." *Los Angeles Times* (March 29, 2016); "What Saudi Farm Companies Are Buying in America." CBS News (March 28, 2016).

4 Richard H. Sanger, "Ibn Saud's Program for Arabia." *Middle East Journal* 1, no. 2 (1947), 180.

5 Karl S. Twitchell, *Saudi Arabia, With an Account of the Development of Its Natural Resources* (New York: Greenwood Press, 1969), 44.

6 Ibid., 44–5.

7 "Telegram: Hull to the Secretary of State to the Minister in Egypt (Kirk)" (February 6, 1942), 890F.61A/2, United States Department of State, *Foreign Relations of the United States: Diplomatic Papers, 1942: The Near East and Africa, Volume IV,* (Washington, DC: US Government Printing Office), 563.

8 Memo, "The Under Secretary of State (Welles) to President Roosevelt," 890F.001 Ibn Saud /3 0, Washington, February 12, 1942. *Foreign Relations of the United States Diplomatic Papers, 1942. The Near East and Africa, Volume IV* (Washington, DC: US Government Printing Office, 1942), 562–3.

9 Twitchell, *Saudi Arabia (1969 edition),* 45.

10 Parker T. Hart, *Saudi Arabia and the United States: Birth of a Security Partnership* (Bloomington: Indiana University Press, 1998), 29.

11 Ahmed Omar Fakry and Karl S. Twitchell, *Report of the United States Agricultural Mission to Saudi Arabia* (Cairo, 1943).

12 K.S. Twitchell, Personal diaries, "U.S. Agricultural Mission to Saudi Arabia," Vol. II–IV. Princeton University Special Collections, Karl S. Twitchell Papers, 1911–1967, Box 7, Folder 5.

13 K.S. Twitchell, "7/31/42, Friday, El Kharj." Personal diaries, "U.S. Agricultural Mission to Saudi Arabia," Vol. II, p.17. Princeton University Special Collections, Karl S. Twitchell Papers, 1911–1967, Box 7, Folder 5.

14 Ibid., 99.

15 Hart, *Saudi Arabia,* 29.

16 Nils E. Lind, "Report on the United States Agricultural Mission at Al Kharj," Enclosure to Despatch No. 108 (April 15, 1945) from American Legation, Jidda, Saudi Arabia. US National Archives and

Records Administration (NARA), Records of the Foreign Service Posts of the Department of State, 1788–1964, RG 84.121.8, 1945, Dhahran Post Files, Box 683, p. 1.

17 Ibid., 4–5.
18 Hart, *Saudi Arabia,* 30.
19 Hart, *Saudi Arabia,* 30–1.
20 "Airgram: The Minister in Saudi Arabia (Eddy) to the Secretary of State" (June 16, 1945), 890F.612/6-1645, United States Department of State, *Foreign relations of the United States: Diplomatic Papers, 1945. The Near East and Africa, Volume VIII.* (Washington, DC: US Government Printing Office, 1945), 907.
21 Ibid., 908.
22 For more accounts of Al Kharj in the 1940s, see Thomas W. Lippman, *Inside the Mirage: America's Fragile Partnership With Saudi Arabia* (Boulder: Westview Press, 2004), 179–99; Chad H. Parker, *Making the Desert Modern: Americans, Arabs, and Oil on the Saudi Frontier, 1933–1973* (Amherst: University of Massachusetts Press, 2015), 91–118; J. E. Peterson, *Saudi Arabia Under Ibn Saud: Economic and Financial Foundations of the State* (New York: I.B. Tauris, 2018), 106–12; Robert Vitalis, *America's Kingdom: Mythmaking on the Saudi Oil Frontier* (Stanford: Stanford University Press, 2007), 70–4; Eckart Woertz, *Oil for Food: The Global Food Crisis and the Middle East* (Oxford: Oxford University Press, 2013), 67–70.
23 Karl S. Twitchell, *Saudi Arabia, With an Account of the Development of Its Natural Resources* (Princeton: Princeton University Press, 1953), 172.
24 Lippman, *Inside the Mirage,* 184; Mildred Montgomery Logan, "I Like Being the Garden of Eden's First Lady." *The Cattleman* 38, no. 5 (October 1951), 108.
25 Sanger, "Ibn Saud's Program," 64; See also Henrietta M. Holm, *The Agricultural Resources of the Arabian Peninsula* (Washington, DC: US Department of Agriculture Foreign Agricultural Service, 1955), 6.
26 Sanger, "Ibn Saud's Program," 62.
27 Nils E. Lind, "Report on the United States Agricultural Mission at Al Kharj," Enclosure to Despatch No. 108 (April 15, 1945) from American Legation, Jidda, Saudi Arabia. US NARA, Records of the Foreign Service Posts of the Department of State, 1788–1964, RG 84.121.8, 1945, Dhahran Post Files, Box 683, 2.
28 Lorania K. Francis, "Arab Farms Boom Under Americans: Output Doubled in Year as Aramco Runs Project on Man-Made Oasis." *Los Angeles Times* (March 28, 1951); Peterson, *Saudi Arabia,* 112; Richard Sanger, *The Arabian Peninsula* (Ithaca: Cornell University

Press, 1954), 66; J.D. Tompkins, "Saudi Arabia's Reclamation Plan Turns Desert Into Fertile Farm." *New York Herald Tribune* (May 16, 1948).

29 Sanger, *The Arabian Peninsula,* 66.

30 George B. Cressey, "Water in the Desert." *Annals of the Association of American Geographers* 47, no. 2 (1957), 106.

31 On its wider history in the US West, see Jack Seitz, "Imagining Alfalfastan: Plant Exploration, Technopolitics, Colonialism, and the Environment in the American West and Russian Central Asia, 1897–1930." *Agricultural History* 95, no. 3 (2021), 444–71.

32 A. J. Wells, *The New Arizona: Homes and Wealth for Out-of-Doors Folks* (San Francisco: Southern Pacific, 1907), 11.

33 Department of State, For the Press, September 24, 1943, No. 404. Princeton University Special Collections, Karl S. Twitchell Papers, 1911–1967, Box 17, Folder 1.

34 Letter from K.S. Twitchell to Paul Alling, Esq., Chief, Division of Near Eastern Affairs, Department of State (September 15, 1943). Princeton University Special Collections, Karl S. Twitchell Papers, 1911–1967, Box 17, Folder 1.

35 "Arabians Learn Navajo Methods" (December 1943), *Desert Magazine:* 33; "Arabian Prince Will Visit Grand Canyon" (October 13, 1943), *Tucson Daily Citizen:* 8; "Saudi Arabia Princes Visit Grand Canyon: Royalty of Kingdom Said to Be Studying Industry in U.S.A." (October 15, 1943), *Winslow Mail:* 1.

36 Letter from J.G. Hamilton to K.S. Twitchell (December 6, 1943). Princeton University Special Collections, Karl S. Twitchell Papers, 1911–1967, Box 4, Folder 7.

37 Twitchell, *Saudi Arabia (1969 edition),* 208.

38 K.S. Twitchell, "5/18/42, Monday, El Kharj." Personal diaries, "U.S. Agricultural Mission to Saudi Arabia," Vol. II, p.12. Princeton University Special Collections, Karl S. Twitchell Papers, 1911–1967, Box 7, Folder 5.

39 "Arabian Prince Will Visit Tucson Shortly." *Tucson Daily Citizen* (January 20, 1947), 1.

40 "Welcome Set for Visitor." *Arizona Republic* (January 23, 1947), 14.

41 "Arabian Crown Prince Due Today in Phoenix." *Arizona Republic* (January 26, 1947), 1–2.

42 Ibid.

43 "Royal Arabian Party Arrives for Inspection Tour of Valley." *Arizona Republic* (January 27, 1947), 3, 5.

44 Jerry McLain, "Arabians Delighted by Tour." *Arizona Republic* (January 28, 1947), 3.

45 "Arabian Visitors End Tour." *Arizona Republic* (January 29, 1947), 2.

46  Sanger, *Arabian Peninsula*, 66.
47  Mildred Logan, "Summary on Al Kharj from Sam T. Logan, Feb. 1985," Georgetown University Special Collections, Mulligan Papers, Box 8, Folder 10: 1.
48  Ibid., 2.
49  Twitchell, *Saudi Arabia (1953 edition)*, 171. See also, Hart, *Saudi Arabia*, 30; Peterson, *Saudi Arabia*, 107; Vitalis, *America's Kingdom*, 70.
50  "Field Audit Report No. 4, Al Kharj Farms 1954" (August 28, 1954), Arabian American Oil Company, Dhahran, Saudi Arabia. Georgetown University Special Collections, Mulligan Papers, Box 8, Folder 10: 30–5.
51  Peterson, *Saudi Arabia*, 107.
52  Toby Craig Jones, *Desert Kingdom: How Oil and Water Forged Modern Saudi Arabia* (Cambridge: Harvard University Press, 2010), 11.
53  Douglas D. Crary, "Recent Agricultural Developments in Saudi Arabia." *Geographical Review* 41, no. 3 (1951), 367.
54  Latham, *The Right Kind of Revolution*, 112. See also Corey Ross, *Ecology and Power in the Age of Empire: Europe and the Transformation of the Tropical World* (Oxford: Oxford University Press, 2017); Vandana Shiva, *The Violence of the Green Revolution: Third World Agriculture, Ecology, and Politics* (London: Zed, 1991).
55  Daniël van der Meulen, *The Wells of Ibn Sa'ud* (New York: Praeger, 1957), 213–14.
56  See also Jones, *Desert Kingdom*; Vitalis, *America's Kingdom*.
57  This is a constant thread running through the Foreign Relations of the United States Diplomatic Papers, but for a review, see Peterson, *Saudi Arabia*.
58  Adam Hanieh, *Money, Markets, and Monarchies: The Gulf Cooperation Council and the Political Economy of the Contemporary Middle East* (New York: Cambridge University Press, 2018), 115.
59  Kristin Fabbe, Safwan Al-Amin, Esel Çekin, and Natalie Kindred. *Almarai Company: Milk and Modernization in the Kingdom of Saudi Arabia* (Cambridge: Harvard Business School, 2018); Hanieh, *Money, Markets*, 128; Laurent A. Lambert, and Hisham Bin Hashim, "A Century of Saudi-Qatari Food Insecurity: Paradigmatic Shifts in the Geopolitics, Economics and Sustainability of Gulf States Animal Agriculture." *The Arab World Geographer* 20, no. 4 (2017), 261–81.
60  Md Rasooldeen, "Almarai's Pursuit of Quality Ensures Unique Success Story." *Arab News* (June 9, 2012); "Operation Almarai,"

National Geographic TV Abu Dhabi (September 17, 2012), natgeotv.com/me/operation-almarai.

61 Christian Gerlach, "Famine Responses in the World Food Crisis 1972–5 and the World Food Conference of 1974." *European Review of History* 22, no. 6 (2015), 930.

62 Howard Bowen-Jones and Roderick Dutton, *Agriculture in the Arabian Peninsula* (London: Economist Intelligence Unit, 1983), 162; Craig Smith, "Al Kharj Journal: Milk Flows From Desert at a Unique Saudi Farm." *New York Times* (December 31, 2002); Woertz, *Oil for Food*, 139.

63 Natalie Koch, "Food as a Weapon? The Geopolitics of Food and the Qatar–Gulf Rift." *Security Dialogue* 52, no. 2 (2021), 118–34.

64 Hanieh, *Money, Markets*; Jones, *Desert Kingdom*; Lambert and Bin Hashim, "A Century"; Lippman, *Inside the Mirage*, 197; Woertz, *Oil for Food*.

65 Elie Elhadj, *Camels Don't Fly, Deserts Don't Bloom: An Assessment of Saudi Arabia's Experiment in Desert Agriculture* (London: Water Issues Study Group, SOAS/King's College London, 2004).

66 Bowen-Jones and Dutton, *Agriculture*, 30.

67 Lippman, *Inside the Mirage*, 196.

68 Vahid Nowshirvani, "The Yellow Brick Road: Self-Sufficiency or Self-Enrichment in Saudi Agriculture?" *MERIP Middle East Report* 145 (1987), 7–13.

69 Hanieh, *Money, Markets*, 118, 127–8; Woertz, *Oil for Food*, 91–2; Eckart Woertz, "The Governance of Gulf Agro-Investments." *Globalizations* 10, no. 1 (2013), 87–104.

70 Fabbe et al., *Almarai Company*; Hanieh, *Money, Markets*, 128; Lambert and Bin Hashim, "A Century."

## 4. Desal

1 Winston Churchill, "Sinews of Peace." *British Information Services* (March 5, 1946). British National Archives FO 371/51624.

2 Daniel Immerwahr, *How to Hide an Empire: A History of the Greater United States* (New York: Farrar, Straus and Giroux, 2019).

3 Latham, *The Right Kind of Revolution*; Carl Bauer and Luis Catalán, "Water, Law, and Development in Chile/California Cooperation, 1960–70s." World Development 90 (2017), 184–98; Richard P. Garlitz, *A Mission for Development: Utah Universities and the Point Four Program in Iran* (Logan: Utah State University Press, 2018); Christopher Sneddon, *Concrete Revolution: Large*

*Dams, Cold War Geopolitics, and the US Bureau of Reclamation* (Chicago: University of Chicago Press, 2015).

4 Latham, *The Right Kind of Revolution*, 36. See Harold D. Lasswell, "The Policy Orientation." In *The Policy Sciences: Recent Developments in Scope and Method*, edited by Daniel Lerner and Harold D. Lasswell (Stanford: Stanford University Press, 1951), 3–43.

5 *Arid Lands Research at the University of Arizona* (Tucson: Office of Arid Lands Studies, 1980), 21. UA Special Collections, E9791 Univ.4.5 A698 A6988.

6 Statement of Welcome by Richard A. Harvill, Arid Lands Conference, June 3, 1969. UA Special Collections, Harvill Presidential Correspondence Files, 1969, Arid Lands–General.

7 On Barak, *Powering Empire: How Coal Made the Middle East and Sparked Global Carbonization* (Oakland: University of California Press, 2020), 42.

8 Michael Christopher Low, "Desert Dreams of Drinking the Sea, Consumed by the Cold War: Transnational Flows of Desalination and Energy From the Pacific to the Persian Gulf." *Environment and History* 26, no. 2 (2020), 145–74.

9 Bertram Thomas, *Arabia Felix: Across the "Empty Quarter" of Arabia* (New York: C. Scribner's Sons, 1932); Harry St. John Bridger Philby, *The Empty Quarter* (New York: H. Holt and Co., 1933); Wilfred Thesiger, *Arabian Sands* (New York: Dutton, 1959).

10 Joseph Hodge, *Triumph of the Expert: Agrarian Doctrines of Development and the Legacies of British Colonialism* (Athens: Ohio University Press, 2007).

11 Matthew MacLean. *Spatial Transformations and the Emergence of "the National": Infrastructures and the Formation of the United Arab Emirates, 1950–1980.* Ph.D. Dissertation (New York: Department of History, New York University, 2017), 30. See also Anna Zacharias, "How the Digdagga Experimental Farm in RAK Revolutionised Regional Agriculture in the 1960s." *National* (August 18, 2017).

12 Mr. A.R. Walmsley to M. Gale, Esq., Bahrain, July 19, 1957. FO 371/126956, EA 1281/5. "Development of Agriculture in Trucial States." Arabian Gulf Digital Archive.

13 Howard Bowen-Jones, "Agriculture in Bahrain, Kuwait, Qatar and UAE." In *Issues in Development: The Arab Gulf States*, edited by May Ziwar-Daftari (London: MD Research and Services, 1980), 46–64; Howard Bowen-Jones and Roderick Dutton, *Agriculture in the Arabian Peninsula* (London: Economist Intelligence Unit, 1983); Ragaei El Mallakh, "The Challenge of Affluence: Abu Dhabi." *Middle East Journal* 24, no. 2 (1970), 135–46; Ragaei El

Mallakh, *The Economic Development of the United Arab Emirates* (New York: St. Martin's Press, 1981).

14 University of Arizona Special Collections, UA Bio, Hodges, Carl N. 1937–, Printed Materials. Hodges' CV updates filed with the university are inconsistent regarding his field of graduate study, which is sometimes named as meteorology, atmospheric physics, or water resources administration.

15 "Sun, Sand, and Sea." National Education Television and KUAT-TV, *Spectrum* 29 (1965). This can be viewed online at americanarchive.org.

16 Mari N. Jensen, "In Memoriam: Richard Kassander, UA's First VP for Research." *UA@Work* (September 19, 2017).

17 Sam Negri, "Carl Hodges and the ERL: A Wunderkind at the Wonderworks." *Arizona Highways* 63, no. 5 (May 1987), 12–18. On the OSW, see Low, "Desert Dreams."

18 University of Arizona Special Collections, Harvill Presidential Correspondence Files, 1968–69, Atmospheric Physics-General.

19 "Technology: Diesels in the Desert." *Time* 90, no. 10 (September 8, 1967), 32.

20 Robert J. Bazell, "Arid Land Agriculture: Shaikh Up in Arizona Research." *Science* 171, no. 3975 (1971), 989. See also Carl N. Hodges, "Desert Food Factories." *Technology Review* 77, no. 3 (1975), 33–9; Negri, "Carl Hodges." Elsewhere, the connection with Sheikh Zayed is described not as resulting from the magazine article, but from a meeting Hayes had in Kuwait with one of Zayed's advisers while on a 17-country tour to promote the greenhouse/desalting plant in Mexico, e.g., "Tilling the desert under plastic skies." *Business Week* (May 9, 1970), 92–4.

21 Nyla Crone, "UA Team to Build Arabian Plant." *Tucson Daily Citizen* (February 27, 1969), 25.

22 C. Hillinger, "Gardens in the Desert: Sheik Looks to the Future." *Willoughby News Herald* (May 14, 1969), 22.

23 D. Perlman, "High Promise for Desert Coasts: Sea Water Food Factory." *San Francisco Chronicle* (February 16, 1970) 10.

24 Department of State to Amembassies Cairo, Jidda, Kuwait, New Delhi, Rawalpindi, Tehran, Tripoli, Tel Aviv, Tunis, Airgram CA-1742, March 26, 1970, file SCI 6-1 TRUCIAL ST, 1970–73, Subject-Numeric File, RG 59: General Records of the Department of State, US National Archives (RG 59, USNA).

25 Ibid., 6; Crone, "UA Team," 25.

26 B. Thomas, "UofA Official Denies Any Conflict of Interest." *Arizona Republic* (October 19, 1969), 51.

27 E. Finkelstein, "UA Sets Abu Dhabi Table. *Tucson Daily Citizen* (August 18, 1972), 14.

28 Latham, *The Right Kind*, 110.

29 J. Cook, "From the Big Greenhouse in Tucson to the Sands of Abu Dhabi." *Arizona Republic* (November 2, 1969); Finkelstein, "It Can Be Done in a Sand Dune." *Arizona Republic* (March 4, 1970); B. Thomas, "Lush Fruit Growing in Sand Signals Wasteland Conquest." *Arizona Republic* (March 28, 1969).

30 Bowen-Jones, "Agriculture"; Pernilla Ouis, "'Greening the Emirates': The Modern Construction of Nature in the United Arab Emirates." *Cultural Geographies* 9, no. 3 (2002), 334–47.

31 Ouis, "'Greening the Emirates,'" 339.

32 Nyla Crone, "Today's Citizen: UA Scientist Owes Career to His Allergy to Horses. *Tucson Daily Citizen* (July 31, 1970), 27. For example of Hodges using the expression, see Negri, "Carl Hodges," 15.

33 Hodges, "Desert Food Factories," 35.

34 Michael Frenchman. "The Desert Yields Rich Food Crop—at a Price." *The Times* VIII (December 21, 1971).

35 Bowen-Jones and Dutton, *Agriculture*, 158.

36 Cook, "UA Team."

37 Letter from Sayed M.H. Juma (D.G. Planning & Coordination for the State of Abu Dhabi) to UA President Richard A. Harvill, December 28, 1968, Letter No. 348/68, University of Arizona Special Collections, Harvill Presidential Correspondence Files, 1970–1971, Environmental Research Center.

38 Department of State Memorandum of Conversation, "Power/Water/Food Project in Abu Dhabi," August 19, 1970, file POL 33 PERSIAN GULF, 1970–73, RG 59, USNA.

39 Ibid.

40 Letter from Carl Hodges to Senator Paul J. Fannin, September 28, 1970, file POL 7, TRUCIAL ST, 1970–73, RG 59, USNA.

41 Amconsul Dharan to Department of State, Telegram 197526, December 3, 1970, file SCI 6-1 TRUCIAL ST, 1970–73, RG 59, USNA, 1.

42 Ibid., 2.

43 Ibid., 3.

44 Amconsul Dharan to Department of State, Telegram 201363, December 10, 1970, file SCI 6-1 TRUCIAL ST, 1970–73, RG 59, USNA

45 For the loan documents and extensive correspondence on this, see UA Special Collections, Harvill Presidential Correspondence Files, 1970–1971, Environmental Research Center. Further information on the loan is available in file FN 6-1 TRUCIAL ST, 1970–73, RG 59, USNA. For a rare example of public exposure on one aspect of the (many) financial irregularities of the Abu Dhabi project, see Thomas, "UofA Official."

46 Amconsul Dharan to Department of State, Telegram 201363, December 10, 1970, file SCI 6-1 TRUCIAL ST, 1970–73, RG 59, USNA.

47 Tancred Bradshaw, *The End of Empire in the Gulf: From Trucial States to United Arab Emirates* (New York: I.B. Tauris, 2019); James Onley, *Britain and the Gulf Shaikhdoms, 1820–1971: The Politics of Protection* (Doha: Center for International and Regional Studies, Georgetown University School of Foreign Service in Qatar, 2009).

48 Letter from President John P. Schaefer to Khalifa Al-Yusef, Chairman, Arid Lands Research Center Committee, Abu Dhabi (July 14, 1971). UA Special Collections, Schaefer Presidential Correspondence Files, 1971–1972, Environmental Research Center.

49 Merle Jensen, "Sadiyat: A Miracle in the Arabian Desert Fifty Years: Then & Now." Lecture at Controlled Agriculture Environmental Center, CALS, University of Arizona (September 27, 2019).

50 Letter from Hodges to Sheikh Hadif bin Humaid, 14 September 1973. UA Special Collections, Schaefer Presidential Correspondence Files.

51 Anonymous interview, Abu Dhabi, UAE, February 2019.

52 Roger L. Geiger, *Research and Relevant Knowledge: American Research Universities Since World War II* (New York: Oxford University Press, 1993), 273–83.

53 Sarah Townsend, "Abu Dhabi Rolls Out Dh 1bn Incentive Scheme in Support of Agri-Tech Companies", *National* (March 11, 2019); Mariam Al Mheiri, "Technology Will Make the UAE One of the World's Most Food-Secure Countries by 2021." *National* (January 16, 2019).

## 5. Dreams

1 John Allen and Mark Nelson, *Space Biospheres* (Malabar: Orbit, 1987), 1.

2 Rachel Carson, *Silent Spring* (Boston: Houghton Mifflin, 1962); Paul R. Ehrlich, *The Population Bomb* (New York: Ballantine Books, 1968).

3 Frederick Buell, "A Short History of Environmental Apocalypse." In *Future Ethics: Climate Change and Apocalyptic Imagination*, edited by Stefan Skrimshire (London: Continuum, 2010), 20.

4 Alvin Toffler, *Future Shock* (New York: Random House, 1970).

5 Patrick McCray, "California Dreamin': Visioneering the Technological Future." In *Where Minds and Matters Meet: Technology in California and the West*, edited by Volker Janssen

(Berkeley: University of California Press, 2012); Patrick McCray, *The Visioneers: How a Group of Elite Scientists Pursued Space Colonies, Nanotechnologies, and a Limitless Future* (Princeton: Princeton University Press, 2012).

6 McCray, "California Dreamin'," 370.

7 Paolo Soleri and Lissa McCullough, *Conversations with Paolo Soleri* (New York: Princeton Architectural Press, 2012), 34.

8 Paolo Soleri, *Arcology, the City in the Image of Man* (Cambridge: MIT Press, 1969).

9 Sam Lubell, "Roughing It in Arcosanti, Arizona, a Sci-Fi Mini City Said to Have Inspired 'Star Wars.'" *Los Angeles Times*. (November 14, 2015).

10 Lubell, "Roughing It."

11 Soleri, *Arcology.*

12 Frank Herbert, *Dune* (Philadelphia: Chilton Books, 1965). See Daniel Immerwahr, "Heresies of 'Dune.'" *Los Angeles Review of Books* (November 19, 2020); Daniel Immerwahr, "The Quileute *Dune*: Frank Herbert, Indigeneity, and Empire." *Journal of American Studies* 56, no. 2 (2022): 191-216; Hari Kunzru, "*Dune*, 50 Years On: How a Science Fiction Novel Changed the World." *Guardian* (July 3, 2015).

13 Kunzru, "*Dune.*"

14 Carl N. Hodges, "Desert Food Factories." *Technology Review* 77, no. 3 (1975), 35.

15 T. E. Lawrence, *The Seven Pillars of Wisdom* (New York: G.H. Doran, 1926); Wilfred Thesiger, *Arabian Sands* (New York: Dutton, 1959). See Roxana Hadadi, "*Dune* Has a Desert Problem." *Vulture.com* (October 29, 2021); Kara Kennedy, "Lawrence of Arabia, Paul Atreides, and the Roots of Frank Herbert's *Dune.*" *Tor.com* (June 2, 2021).

16 Kunzru, "*Dune.*"

17 Rothe, "Governing the End," 146.

18 Andrew Curley and Majerle Lister, "Already Existing Dystopias: Tribal Sovereignty, Extraction, and Decolonizing the Anthropocene." In *Handbook on the Changing Geographies of the State: New Spaces of Geopolitics*, edited by Sami Moisio, Natalie Koch, Andrew E.G. Jonas, Christopher Lizotte and Juho Luukkonen (Northampton: Edward Elgar, 2020), 260.

19 Buell, "A Short History"; Sasha Lilley, David McNally, Eddie Yuen, and James Davis, *Catastrophism: The Apocalyptic Politics of Collapse and Rebirth* (Oakland: PM Press, 2012); McCray, *The Visioneers;* Delf Rothe, "Governing the End Times? Planet Politics and the Secular Eschatology of the Anthropocene." *Millennium* 48, no. 2 (2020), 143–64; Stefan Skrimshire, *Future Ethics:*

*Climate Change and Apocalyptic Imagination* (London: Continuum, 2010).

20  Rothe, "Governing the End," 151.

21  Erickson, "Anthropocene Futures," 112.

22  Tim Jackson, "Billionaire Space Race: The Ultimate Symbol of Capitalism's Flawed Obsession With Growth." *Conversation* (July 20, 2021).

23  K. Maria D. Lane, *Geographies of Mars: Seeing and Knowing the Red Planet* (Chicago: University of Chicago Press, 2011).

24  M. Fulmer, "A Look at Flagstaff, Arizona, Where Apollo 11 Astronauts Trained Before Landing on the Moon." *Los Angeles Times* (July 1, 2018); Steve Ranson, "Apollo Astronauts Conducted Desert Survival Training North of Fallon in 1960s." *Lahontan Valley News* (July 20, 2019).

25  "When Astronauts Roamed the Desert." *Desert Oracle* (Summer 2015), 26–7.

26  Quoted in David Kelly, "Life on Mars Gets a Test Run in the Utah Desert." *Los Angeles Times* (June 23, 2019).

27  Jason N. Dittmer, "Colonialism and Place Creation in *Mars Pathfinder* Media Coverage." *Geographical Review* 97, no. 1 (2007), 125.

28  R. Buckminster Fuller, *Operating Manual for Spaceship Earth* (Carbondale: Southern Illinois University Press, 1969), 18.

29  Quoted in Carl Zimmer, "The Lost History of One of the World's Strangest Science Experiments." *New York Times* (March 29, 2019).

30  Founded in 1969, it still operates today as a conference center and farm: synergiaranch.com.

31  Marc Cooper, "The Profits of Doom: The Biospherians Lure Scientists to a High-Priced Feast Under Glass." *Phoenix New Times* (June 19, 1991); Zimmer, "The Lost History."

32  David A. Conrad, "The Eclipse of the Century: A Story of Science, Money, and Culture in Saharan Africa and the American Southwest." *Journal of the Southwest* 56, no. 4 (2014), 606.

33  Conrad, "The Eclipse"; Lane, *Geographies of Mars*; George Webb, *Science in the American Southwest: A Topical History* (Tucson: University of Arizona Press, 2002).

34  Allen and Nelson, *Space Biospheres*.

35  Cooper, "The Profits of Doom."

36  Ibid.

37  Cooper, "The Profits of Doom"; Trufelman, "Biosphere"; Avery Trufelman, "Biosphere: The Theater of Utopia." *Nice Try! Podcast, Curbed* (July 11, 2019); Zimmer, "The Lost History."

38  Anonymous interviews, December 2018–February 2019.

39  Bill Dempster, "Biosphere 2 was science, not a stunt." *Motherboard, Tech by Vice* (June 24, 2017).

40  See for example, Mark Nelson, *Pushing Our Limits: Insights From Biosphere 2* (Tucson: The University of Arizona Press, 2018); Jane Poynter, *The Human Experiment: Two Years and Twenty Minutes Inside Biosphere 2* (New York: Thunder's Mouth Press, 2006); Rebecca Reider, *Dreaming the Biosphere: The Theater of All Possibilities* (Albuquerque: University of New Mexico Press, 2009).

41  Mark Nelson, "Into the Biosphere—Lessons From One of Science's Most Audacious Experiments, *Geographical* (September 4, 2018).

42  Ibid.

43  J. Eubank, "Tales From the Morgue: Locked In at Biosphere II." *Arizona Daily Star* (September 25, 2018).

44  Cooper, "The Profits of Doom"; Zimmer, "The Lost History."

45  Karen Arensen, "Columbia University Ends Its Association With Biosphere 2." *New York Times* (September 9, 2003); Tim Murphy, "Trump's Campaign CEO Ran a Secretive Sci-Fi Project in the Arizona Desert." *Mother Jones* (August 26, 2016); Tim Steller, "Political Notebook: Trump Point Man's Bullying Goes Back to Biosphere." *Arizona Daily Star* (August 25, 2019); Elizabeth Trembath-Reichert, "Biosphere 2 Now for Sale to Highest Bidder." *Columbia Spectator* (February 4, 2005); Zimmer, "The Lost History."

46  "Christopher T. Bannon." *OpenPayrolls.com.*

47  Quoted in UA Research, Discovery and Innovation, "$30M Gift Announced for UA's Biosphere 2." *UA News* (September, 20, 2017).

48  Quoted in Hassan Hijazi, "Biosphere 2 to Have a Permanent Home With the UA." *UA News* (June 27, 2011).

49  Dempster, "Biosphere 2 was science."

50  "About." *Sam at B2.* samb2.space.

51  "Distinguished Arizona Global Alumni." *UA Global,* global. arizona.edu.

52  "Peter Smith, Principal Investigator and Project Leadership, University of Arizona." *Phoenix Mars Mission.* phoenix.lpl.arizona. edu.

53  "Phoenix Mars Lander." *NASA,* nasa.gov.

54  Tim Vanderpool, "World Under Glass: Research That Matters." *UA Alumni Association* (Spring/Summer 2012). arizonaalumni. com. This story was expanded on through an anonymous interview, January 2020.

55  Kareem Shaheen, "First UAE Mars Mission Aims to Inspire a New Generation of Space Scientists." *National Geographic* (July 20, 2020).

56 "Mars 2117." *Mohammed bin Rashid Space Centre.* mbrsc.ae. See Jörg Matthias Determann, *Space Science and the Arab World: Astronauts, Observatories and Nationalism in the Middle East* (New York: I.B. Tauris, 2018), 155–164.

57 Gökçe Günel, *Spaceship in the Desert: Energy, Climate Change, and Urban Design in Abu Dhabi* (Durham: Duke University Press, 2019).

58 Federico Cugurullo, "Urban Eco-Modernisation and the Policy Context of New Eco-City Projects: Where Masdar City Fails and Why." *Urban Studies* 53, no. 11 (2016), 2417–33; Anthony Flint, "What Abu Dhabi's City of the Future Looks Like Now." *Bloomberg CityLab* (February 14, 2020); Katie Herzog, "The World's First Zero-Carbon City is a Big Failure." *Grist* (February 17, 2016); Laura Mallonee, "Inside Masdar City, the UAE's Zero-Carbon City That Will Never Be." *Wired* (June 16, 2016).

59 Gökçe Günel, "Inhabiting the Spaceship: The Connected Isolation of Masdar City." In *Climates: Architecture and the Planetary Imaginary*, edited by James Graham (New York: Lars Müller, 2016), 364.

60 Quoted in Günel, "Inhabiting the Spaceship," 367.

61 Natalie Koch, "Urban 'Utopias': The Disney Stigma and Discourses of 'False Modernity.'" *Environment and Planning A* 44, no. 10 (2012), 2445–62; Donald McNeill, "In Search of the Global Architect: The Case of Norman Foster (and Partners)." *International Journal of Urban and Regional Research* 29, no. 3 (2005), 501–15; Leslie Sklair, *The Icon Project: Architecture, Cities, and Capitalist Globalization* (New York: Oxford University Press, 2017).

62 Harriet Bulkeley and Vanesa Castán Broto, "Government by Experiment? Global Cities and the Governing of Climate Change." *Transactions of the Institute of British Geographers* 38, no. 3 (2013), 361–75.

63 L. Chase Smith, "Technologies of California's Fantasy Future at the 1915 San Diego Panama-California Exposition." In *Where Minds and Matters Meet: Technology in California and the West*, edited by Volker Janssen (Berkeley: University of California Press, 2012), 29.

64 Curley and Lister, "Already Existing Dystopias."

## 6. Deserts

1 Randall Henderson and J. Wilson McKenney, "Editorial: There Are Two Deserts." *Desert Magazine* 1 (1937), 5. For an account of these two traditions in American writing, see Patricia Nelson

Limerick, *Desert Passages: Encounters With the American Deserts* (Albuquerque: University of New Mexico, 1985).

2  Immerwahr, *How to Hide an Empire*; Jodi A. Byrd, *The Transit of Empire: Indigenous Critiques of Colonialism* (Minneapolis: University of Minnesota Press, 2011).

3  Ofelia Zepeda, "Not the Intent of This Desert." *ArtSource Arizona* 6 (2021), 14.

# Index

map of, xii
Muscat, as center of Arabian date
 exporting, 43
Muscat date palm research laboratory,
 23–4
UA's building of date palm laboratory
 in, 56
*Operating Manual for Spaceship Earth*
 (Fuller), 141–2
Oracle, Arizona, site of Biosphere 2, 132*f*
Oregon Territory, 7*f*
O'Toole, John, 119*f*

Pearce, Peter Jon, 143
Philby, St. John, 102
Philecology Foundation, 150
Pima, agricultural systems of, 36, 38
*The Population Bomb* (Ehrlich), 133, 137
Porter, David D., 5, 6
pseudo-scientific propaganda, 134

Qaboos bin Said al Said, 24
Qafishheh, Hamdi, 119*f*
Qatar, map of, xii
Quartzsite, Arizona
 description of as of 2019, 13–14, 18
 Hi Jolly as living out his days in, 13
 Hi Jolly's last camp in, 1, 2*f*, 14
Quast, Karl, 70

race, as at center of how settlement and
 territorial incorporation was viewed
 from Washington, 34
racial bigotry, in early American
 expansionism, 35
racism
 in *Lamp in the Desert* (Martin), 33
 masquerading as benevolence, 32
 on UA campus, 33
Ras Al-Khaimah, Agricultural Trials
 Station in Digdagga, 102–3
Rashid bin Saeed Al Maktoum (sheikh),
 118*f*
reverse osmosis (RO) technology, 100
Riley, James, 118*f*, 119*f*
Robbins, Robert, 33
Rogers, David A., 69–71, 72, 73, 74, 75,
 78, 81–2, 83, 86, 92
Roosevelt, Franklin D., 65–6, 69–70, 71,
 79
Ruiz, Joaquin, 150

Saadiyat Island, Abu Dhabi, greenhouse
 facilities on, 116, 118*f*, 119*f*, 125, 126
"Sahara" trope, 12
Salt River Valley
 agricultural wonders of, 82
 dates as profitable crop in, 52
 publication on (1885), 40–1
SAM (Space Analog for the Moon and
 Mars), 151

Sanderson, Rahleigh, 70
*San Francisco Chronicle*, article on ERL
 Abu Dhabi plant, 110
*San Francisco Evening Bulletin*, article on
 arrival of camel caravan in California,
 12–13
Sanger, Richard, 64, 74, 76
Saud (king), 84, 85
Saud al Saud (prince), 81–4, 82*f*, 84*f*
Saudi Arabia
 Agricultural Mission to (1942), 63, 65,
 66, 69, 88
 as building "modern" state, 86
 dairy farms in, 84–5
 date production in, 24
 decimation of aquifers in, 90, 91
 food crisis in, 90
 history of ties between Arizona and, 62
 map of, xii
 as one of world's largest wheat
 exporters, 90
 as phasing out domestic grain
 production, 91–2
 powerful agricultural lobby in, 91
 transformation of domestic food
 production, 91
 US-based oil companies as receiving
 drilling concessions in, 62–3
Schaeffer, John, 124, 126
*Scientific American*, article about dates as
 staple American product, 52
scientists
 arid empire as privileging white male
 scientists, 134–5, 140
 as hero figures, 151
 Western scientists as colonial heroes/
 planetary managers, 140
 Western scientists as neglecting harm
 they inflicted on natural environment
 and its non-white residents, 140
Seif, Mohammed Mijrin, 119*f*
self-sustaining ecology, Biosphere 2
 presented as example of, 145
Shakhbut (sheikh), 112
*Silent Spring* (Carson), 133, 137
Smith, Peter, 152
Smythe, William, 36
Solar Energy Research Laboratory, later
 Environmental Research Laboratory
 (ERL), 100, 104–7, 105*f*
Soleri, Paolo, 135
Space Analog for the Moon and Mars
 (SAM), 151
*Space Biospheres* (Allen and Nelson), 132
Space Biospheres Ventures, 143, 146, 148,
 149
space race
 billionaire space race, 140
 in Cold War, 143
Spaceship Earth project, 142, 143, 147,
 156